A FEAST OF SEASONS

A Feast of Seasons

Margot R Hodson

**Monarch
Books**
Olive Press

Copyright © Margot R Hodson 2000.
The right of Margot R Hodson to be identified
as author of this work has been asserted by her in
accordance with the Copyright, Designs
and Patents Act 1988.

First published by Monarch Books 2000

ISBN 1 85424 473 6

All rights reserved.
No part of this publication may be reproduced or
transmitted in any form or by any means, electronic
or mechanical, including photocopy, recording or any
information storage and retrieval system, without
permission in writing from Monarch Books,
Concorde House, Grenville Place,
Mill Hill, London NW7 3SA.

Unless otherwise stated, Scripture quotations are
taken from the Holy Bible, New International Version,
copyright © 1973, 1978, 1984 by the International Bible Society.
Used by permission of Hodder and Stoughton Ltd.
All rights reserved.

British Library Cataloguing Data
A catalogue record for this book is available
from the British Library.

Cover Photos:
Pomegranates in Israel, M J Hodson
*Orthodox boy selects his four species for the
Feast of Tabernacles* and *Grapes*, DayStar Images

Designed and produced for the publishers by
Bookprint Creative Services
P.O. Box 827, BN21 3YJ, England.
Printed in Great Britain.

This book is dedicated to
the memory of Ronald Adeney who gave me so much
encouragement. Loved and respected by Jews and Arabs
alike, Ronald served as a priest and teacher in Israel for most
of his life. He is remembered as a wonderful friend, a wise
adviser and a tremendous example in prayer.

ACKNOWLEDGEMENTS

Many people have contributed to this book. First, I would like to thank all those who were part of the Messianic community, Beit Shalom in North London, in the 1990s. We went through a period of our lives together and I have drawn on that experience in writing this book. Next, thanks are due to those many friends in Israel whose hospitality has given me insights into Israeli life. Thirdly, I should thank Charles Hundley and John Wood, who took considerable time to read drafts of this book and made valuable suggestions; and Eira B. Goldsworthy, who made beautiful pictures of each of the crafts. Monarch Publishers have been very helpful at every stage. A special 'thank you' goes to my Mum for trying out the recipes. Finally, I wish to thank my husband, Martin, for enthusiastically entering into a Hebraic approach to Christianity, being flexible when book writing took over our home, constructing the festival diagram, as well as reading the proofs and sampling the recipes. Without Martin's encouragement I would never have finished this project.

CONTENTS

Glossary   9

Chapter One: An invitation to the feasts   19
Chapter Two: Passover – sacrificed for us   31
Chapter Three: Pentecost – first fruits of the harvest   67
Chapter Four: Rosh Hashanah – a trumpet call into the presence of God   87
Chapter Five: Yom Kippur – a time to pray   101
Chapter Six: Tabernacles – Jesus coming among us   119
Chapter Seven: Hanukkah – a festival of lights   141
Chapter Eight: Tu b'Shvat – care for creation   151
Chapter Nine: Purim – delivered from our enemies   161
Chapter Ten: Sabbath – rest and prayer with the family   173
Chapter Eleven: As the seasons close   201

Bibliography   209
Index   213

ABBREVIATIONS

REV The Revised English Bible with Apocrypha (1989) Oxford University Press and Cambridge University Press.
RSV The Holy Bible, Revised Standard Version (1965) Division of Christian Education of the National Council of the Churches of Christ in the United States of America.

GLOSSARY

Afikomen

A piece of unleavened bread that is broken and hidden at the start of a Passover meal. It is found and eaten at the end of the meal, just before the Redemption cup is drunk.

Ashkenazi

Jewish people originating from Germany and northern Europe.

Bar Kockba

Leader of the Jewish uprising in Israel in AD 132. He assumed the name Bar Kockba, which means 'Son of a Star'.

Bar Mitzvah

Bar Mitzvah means 'Son of the Commandment' and is when a young male takes on the responsibility for keeping the Law or Torah. Bar Mitzvah traditionally occurs on the first Sabbath after a boy's thirteenth birthday. In Reform Judaism Bar Mitzvah occurs at the nearest Shavuot to a boy's thirteenth birthday and a parallel 'Bat Mitzvah' is available for girls.

Bikkurim

Hebrew for 'First Fruits'. Seven fruits were commanded to be offered at the Temple each year (Deuteronomy 8:8 and 26:1–11).

Etrog

Thought to be the fruit of the goodly tree mentioned in Leviticus 23:40 as one of the four species to be used at Sukkot. It resembles a large lemon, with a prominent tip or 'pittom'.

Gemara

Aramaic for 'Learning'. This book was completed by the fifth century AD and is a record of rabbinic discussions on the Mishnah in both the Palestinian and Babylonian schools. The Mishnah and Gemara together are known as the Talmud.

Haftorah

A reading from the Prophets selected to fit the weekly Torah reading in the synagogue lectionary.

Haggadah

The liturgy for the Passover Meal.

Hagigah

This was a lamb sacrificed as a peace offering on the second night of Passover.

Hallel

This comprises of Psalms 113–118, and can for some occasions include Psalm 136. It is sung at Passover, Pentecost, Hanukkah and at the Feast of Tabernacles.

Hanukkah

Hebrew for 'Dedication', this is a mid-winter festival to celebrate the rededication of the Temple after the defeat of the Syrian Greeks by the Maccabees in 165 BC.

Hanukkiah

An eight (nine) branched candlestick used at Hanukkah. Over eight days, one extra candle is lit each night by the ninth candle known as the 'Shamash' or Servant. It is sometimes called a Hanukkah Menorah.

Hasmoneans

The dynasty founded by the Maccabees. This was a priestly family and belonged to the Sadducees.

Havdalah

A ceremony to end Shabbat. The word means 'separation' and it marks the separation between the sacred and the secular.

Hillel

One of the senior rabbis teaching at the Temple when Jesus was a child.

Hosannah Rabbah

The seventh day of Tabernacles.

Huppah

A canopy used for a Jewish wedding and symbolising the home.

Kabbalah

A mystical branch of Judaism originating from Babylon and developed in the Middle Ages. Safed in Galilee became a key centre for Kabbalah.

Ketubah

A Jewish marriage document, which states the obligations of a husband to his wife.

Kiddush

A ceremony involving wine and bread each Sabbath. Blessings are recited for each and the bread is eaten after being dipped in salt.

Kittel

A white ceremonial garment worn at Passover and Yom Kippur and sometimes at other festivals. It is a symbol of purity.

Kippah (pl kippot)

A male head covering usually in the form of a small skull cap.

Kol Nidrei

Hebrew for 'All Vows'. It is a service on the eve of Yom Kippur for the cancellation of religious vows.

Kosher

Food prepared in accordance with Jewish ritual food laws. Pork and shellfish are forbidden and it is not possible to mix milk and meat.

Lag b'Omer

A festival that breaks the mourning period between Passover and Pentecost.

Lulav

Hebrew for 'Palm Branch', it is one of the four species used at Sukkot.

Matzah

Unleavened bread used at Passover. Modern Matzah is wafer thin and dry. It is usually square shaped and pierced with holes.

Megillah

Hebrew for 'Scroll', this is the name for the book of Esther and the tractate in the Mishnah concerning the festival of Purim.

Menorah

The seven-branched candlestick kept in the Holy Place in the Temple. Today the Menorah is a common Jewish symbol, though it is traditional not to light a replica out of respect for the original Menorah in the Temple.

Messianic Jews

The most widely accepted modern name for Jewish believers in Jesus. The terms Hebrew Christian and Jewish Christian are also used. It is most courteous to use the preferred term chosen by an individual.

Mikvah (pl Mikvot)

A Jewish ritual bath, usually located at the synagogue.

Mishnah

Hebrew for 'Teaching', this is a book recording the debates on Jewish oral law. It was compiled by the third century AD and is in some senses a commentary on the Old Testament.

Omer

The barley offering on the second day of Passover. This also marks the start of a period of counting for 50 days (counting the Omer) that ends with the feast of Pentecost.

Pesach

Hebrew for Passover, the name derives from the action of the Lord in passing over the protected Hebrew homes before the Exodus from Egypt.

Pharisees

One of the main groups of Jews in the Second Temple (New Testament) period. Pharisees believed in the resurrection and were very devoted to the Bible.

Purim

Hebrew for 'Lots' and the Hebrew name for the Feast of Esther.

Rosh Hashanah

Literally 'Head of the Year', this is the New Year of the Jewish calander.

Sadducees

One of the main groups of Jews in the Second Temple (New Testament) period. These were mostly affluent priestly families. Sadducees did not believe in the resurrection and centred their worship on Temple sacrifice.

Sanhedrin

The Jewish ruling council in the Second Temple (New Testament) period.

Seder

Hebrew for 'Order', this describes the instructions for the ceremony on Passover night. The Passover meal and the accompanying ceremony is often simply called a Seder.

Sephardi

Jewish people and communities originating from Spain, the Mediterranean and the Middle East.

Septuagint

A translation of the Hebrew scriptures into Greek in the second century BC.

Shabbat

The Jewish Sabbath, lasting from sundown on Friday until sundown on Saturday.

Shammai

One of the two great rabbinic teachers at, or just before, the time of Jesus.

Shavuot

Hebrew for 'Weeks', this is the Jewish festival of Pentecost.

Shofar

A ram's horn, blown on ceremonial occasions.

Simchat Torah

Hebrew for 'rejoicing in the law', and the eighth day after the start of the Feast of Tabernacles. This is a post-biblical festival and probably dates from the tenth century.

Sukkah

Hebrew for 'Shelter'. These are built outside homes for the Feast of Tabernacles.

Sukkot

Hebrew for 'Shelters', this is the Hebrew name for the Feast of Tabernacles.

Talmud

The combined Mishnah and Gemara. There is a Babylonian and a Palestinian Talmud, representing the slightly different debates of these two schools.

Targum

The name of an Aramaic translation of the Hebrew Bible. This sometimes brings further explanation of the text or gives alternative translations.

Tashlich

A Rosh Hashanah tradition of throwing pebbles or bread into a running stream as a sign of repentance.

Teshuvah

Hebrew for 'Repentance'.

Tishah b'Av

Ninth of Av in the Jewish calendar. This is the date when both Solomon's Temple was destroyed in 586 BC and the Second Temple was burned to the ground in AD 70. It is a day of fasting.

Torah

The Pentateuch, the first five books of the Bible.

Tu b'Shvat

The Jewish New Year for trees.

Yeshua

The original Hebrew form of the name 'Jesus'.

Yom h'Atzmaut

The day celebrating Israel's Declaration of Independence on 14 May 1948, which was 5 Iyar in the Jewish calendar.

Yom ha Shoah

Holocaust Memorial Day and on 27 Nissan in the Jewish calendar. This commemorates the six million Jewish people who were murdered in Nazi Europe between 1939 and 1945.

Yom Kippur

Yom Kippur literally means 'Day of Covering', that is, 'Day of Atonement'. It is the most solemn day in the Jewish calendar and is dedicated to fasting and prayer.

Chapter One

AN INVITATION TO THE FEASTS

I would like to invite you to come with me on a journey through the festival year of the Bible. The path is one usually followed by Jewish people and we will explore traditions that began in Old Testament times. Most of these festivals were also celebrated in the New Testament period and would have been familiar to Jesus and his early Jewish followers. By understanding Judaism more fully we will understand the background to the Bible and the Christian faith. As we go through the seasons together we get a feel for the rhythm of the year that Jesus himself knew from childhood. Let us travel with him on our journey through time.

Different types of time

There are two types of time in Judaism.[1] There is historical time that moves on to different things every year. We all need this type of time to grow and change as we go through life, but it is not the only type of time. There is also cyclical time, which goes through the rhythm of the seasons. Every year we experience the cycle of the natural world as spring gives way to summer and summer lengthens into autumn, which finally draws out into winter's cold. Whatever our background, it is likely that there are festivals we associate with these different times of year. Maybe they evoke the aromas of traditional foods, the laughter of games or the melodies of songs. We need this type of time just as much as our linear time. Cyclical time gives us our regularity in life. The festivals are havens where we can each pause for a while to take a breath before moving forward again. For children they make up the landscape of the year and are full of excitement and expectancy. For older people they are anchors to happy memories and familiar companions as life grows slowly towards eternity.

Jewish New Years

Judaism recognises these different types of time by giving each of them a personal New Year.[2] The New Year for years is in the autumn and is marked by the festival Rosh Hashanah, which literally means 'head of the year'. In biblical times this was when the special years would start, such as the Jubilee when slaves were released (Leviticus 25). In modern Judaism it is when the creation of the world is celebrated as the birth of historical time.

Festivals also have their own special New Year and this starts in the spring with Passover. This is the oldest and the greatest of the feasts and begins the story of the festivals, which every year remembers how God fulfilled his covenant relationship with the Jewish people. This is the New Year for kings in the Bible, who counted the years of their reign from this point, regardless of when they started to govern.

There are two smaller New Years in the Jewish calendar. One is for the tithing of animals and is in the summer. There are no special traditions attached to this. The other is the New Year for trees. This is a later Jewish festival that has its roots in the Bible and draws on the biblical teaching concerning our stewardship of nature.

Fellow travellers

To consider Jesus' journey through the festival year it is helpful to get to know his fellow travellers. Who went with him and how did their lives affect his? When many of us think of traditional festivals, we are transported back to childhood. This was when our views of these events were formed and this was where we learnt the traditions that shaped our later lives, usually from our parents.

Jesus' parents were particularly devout for their generation.[3] Mary went to the Temple to offer a sacrifice and give thanks for the birth of Jesus though it was not obligatory for her to go in person.[4] One of the few stories that we have of Jesus' childhood concerns a journey to Jerusalem to celebrate Passover (Luke 2:41–50). Luke explains that Mary and Joseph went up to Jerusalem every year for this festival. This would not have been the case with all Jews living in Galilee and the impact of these regular trips was apparent in Jesus' later life, not least in his familiarity with the city and with the Temple. The disciples in contrast were quite overwhelmed by the Temple on their visit to Jerusalem with him (Mark 13:1).

When he visited Jerusalem at the age of twelve, Jesus, like many children who have a passionate interest that takes over on a holiday, was drawn like a magnet to the Temple courts and the rabbis. This was probably not the only Passover Jesus spent with these scholars and again this showed in adulthood through his knowledge and ability in rabbinic debate. His teachers were the Pharisees, who believed in the resurrection and were very devoted to the Bible, with a developing oral interpretation that had been handed on to them for generations. They did not preach a sermon or give a lecture, but, sitting down, they would invite a question to begin a dialogue with their students. This question and answer method of teaching continued in Judaism and is also a feature of many of the New Testament debates.[5] Christians often see the Pharisees very negatively as people obsessed with the details of the law. Although Jesus challenged the excesses of the more severe and had a distinct agenda from them, he was probably nearer to this group in his views than to any other. Some of his teaching shows the direct influence of Rabbi Hillel, one of the senior rabbis teaching at the Temple when Jesus was a child.[6] There had been a long tradition of pairs of teachers and Hillel was more lenient than his counterpart, Shammai. Hillel came from a wealthy family in Babylon, but gave up everything to study as a poor student in Jerusalem. Even as a famous rabbi, he remained modest and down to earth, usually taking a generous view of the law. Shammai, an engineer, was known for forthright integrity and exactness. He judged himself and others by the strictest possible standards. Hillel's views eventually prevailed in Judaism.[7]

There is a legend that Shammai took up his post after his predecessor had left to join the Essenes.[8] It was members of this group who lived in Qumran where the Dead Sea Scrolls were discovered. They were largely a monastic group and took ritual cleanliness and spiritual purity very seriously. In this and their retreat to the desert, there are similarities between the Essenes and John the Baptist. Though it would be wrong to assume a link, there can be little doubt that John and Jesus would have known of the Essenes and their challenge to the spiritual integrity of the Jewish religious establishment.

The final group to mention are the Sadducees. These were aristocratic, mainly priestly families who lived in the upper city of Jerusalem. Today you can visit a superb excavation of one of their homes in the Jewish Quarter of the Old City. They believed that the Jewish religion entirely centred on the Temple and opposed the Pharisees on almost every major point. They did not believe in life after death, they did not believe in the oral law (the oral interpretation of the Bible), and they did not believe that religion 'belonged to the people'. Jesus also debated with this group and challenged them for not having a thorough understanding of the scriptures (Mark 12:18–27).

Later travellers

The festivals fitted within the cyclical time of the New Testament era and we can learn much about Jesus' world from them. They also developed and changed through historical time and a brief understanding of the major streams within Judaism is important. Who else in history travelled the festival year?

Rabbinic Judaism

After the destruction of the Temple in AD 70, the dispersion of Jewish people around the known world increased. The Sadducees died away as a spiritual force and the Pharisees took Judaism forward. Many scholars fled Jerusalem, including the famous Rabbi Johanan Ben Zakkai. These gathered at Yavneh, a town to the south of Jaffa, and reconvened the Sanhedrin, the Jewish ruling council. Over the next sixty years they rethought and redeveloped Judaism as a religion of the Diaspora without need of a Temple. Much of their thinking was based on the experience of the exile in Babylon, when a synagogue style of worship had become the norm. The Pharisees used the term rabbi or teacher and from this we get the title Rabbinic Judaism.

In AD 132 there was a Jewish uprising under a soldier called Bar Kockba. The revolt failed and the Sanhedrin was forced to move from Yavneh to Tiberias in Galilee. This became a new intellectual centre for Judaism along with the great school of learning that continued in Babylonia. Up until the destruction of the Temple, the written instructions for the feasts were those in the Old Testament. The supplementary traditions for each festival were oral. From a Jewish perspective, this made them a kind of living word that could change and adapt with the needs of each generation. Once the Temple ceased to be a focus for the feasts, the transmission of these traditions became more difficult in a purely oral form and needed to be written down. There were many different points of view regarding the exact way of keeping each festival, and, rather than force a consensus, these different views were recorded side by side. These debates were eventually gathered together with discussions about all the other aspects of Jewish law in about AD 220. The resulting book, called the Mishnah, is in some senses a commentary on the Old Testament and on the whole of Judaism. It is a window through time to the debates on Judaism of the early centuries of our era, and is the key resource for understanding the Judaism of that period.

Both the Babylonian and the Galilean schools continued to debate the Bible and the oral law, now codified in the Mishnah. These debates were recorded over the third to fifth centuries and made another layer of commentary called the Gemara. This, together with the Mishnah, became known as the Talmud. Debates varied in Babylon and the Holy Land and there are two Talmuds, the Babylonian and the Jerusalem or Palestinian Talmud.

Spain, Germany and beyond

As the Jews formed communities in many different parts of the world, so they developed different customs and traditions. By the Middle Ages two main groups had emerged. Sephardi Jews are of a Middle Eastern tradition. These were originally focused on the community in Spain and experienced a golden era for several centuries. Their position became increasingly precarious with the rise of the Inquisition and eventually they were expelled from Spain in 1492. Communities had already begun to grow in other lands and the Sephardim spread across the Mediterranean and Middle East, with a few moving into northern Europe and some striking out to Latin

America. Much of Sephardi tradition has developed in Arab, Muslim lands and shows this influence.

One thread of Jewish learning is a mystical approach known as kabbalah. The origins of this go back to the Babylonian exile and are focused on understanding both the immanence and transcendence of God. After the expulsion from Spain, many Sephardi kabbalists moved to Safed in Galilee and this became a key centre for this form of Judaism.[9]

The other main group is of Ashkenazi Jews. These developed out of the Jewish communities of the Germanic and northern European countries who have flourished over the last thousand years, despite persecution. Though many of their traditions are remarkably similar to the Sephardi communities, demonstrating how much communication went on between the groups, there are significant differences. Most Jewish people living in Britain are of Ashkenazi origin, as are a high percentage of those in North America. Israel used to have a greater Sephardi population, but, in recent years, the very high immigration from Russia has significantly increased the Ashkenazi community. During the eighteenth and nineteenth centuries, Ashkenazi Jews grew into a variety of different groupings. The mainstream became known as Orthodox Jews and still make up the majority of religious Jewish people. In the eighteenth century a movement began in Eastern Europe known as the Hassidim or Pious ones. These were a kind of charismatic movement within Judaism and have grown into the Ultra Orthodox groups of today, distinguished by their traditional Eastern European clothing. In nineteenth-century Germany, Jewish intellectuals wanting more contact with the outside world formed the Reform movement. The Reform and Liberal movements remain strong in Britain and America, though they are still not properly recognised in Israel.[10]

Stages in the cycle

As the cycle of the feasts has developed through historical time so new festivals have been added. The core festivals are those of the Old Testament, or Hebrew Bible, as many people now prefer to describe it. Leviticus 23 sets out the festivals of: Sabbath (Shabbat); Passover (Pesach) and First Fruits (Bikkurim); Pentecost (Shavuot); Trumpets (Rosh Hashanah); Day of Atonement (Yom Kippur) and Tabernacles (Sukkot). Each of these has a Hebrew name (given in brackets) and both names may be used for each festival. The last three of these festivals (Rosh Hashanah, Yom Kippur and Sukkot) come together and are known as the High Holy Days. In Temple times the festival calander developed into the three times in the year when it was commanded to go up to Jerusalem. These 'pilgrimage festivals' were Passover, Pentecost and Tabernacles. The next two festivals to be added, Hanukkah and Purim, probably came from the time just after the Hebrew Bible was completed. They complete the number of festivals that would have been known in the New Testament. All of these festivals have a chapter of their own in this book.

A further layer of festivals came with Lag b'Omer and Tishah b'Av. Lag b'Omer comes between Passover and Pentecost. This is an intense waiting period when many mourning practices are kept. The origins of the day are hazy, though it seems to concern events of the early second century when Bar Kockba led the revolt against the Romans with the support of a famous rabbi, Akiva. One legend is that Akiva's students were dying of plague. The people repented and interceded for them and the plague stopped on this date. A second theory is that it was on this day that Bar Kockba temporarily won back Jerusalem from the Romans. Whatever the origins of Lag b'Omer, it is the one day in this period when mourning can cease. Fasting is forbidden and

The Jewish Year

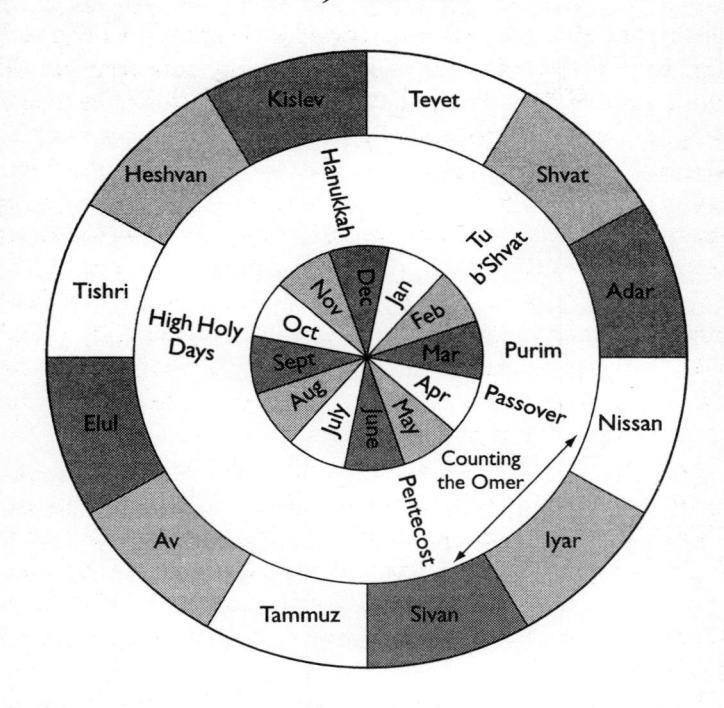

Legend
Outer circle: Jewish months
Middle circle: Jewish festivals
Inner circle: approximate coincidence with Gregorian calendar

marriages are permitted. Tishah b'Av is in August on 9 Av in the Jewish calendar. This is the date when both Solomon's Temple was destroyed in 586 BC and the Second Temple was burned to the ground in AD 70. Ever since, religious Jewish people have fasted on this day.

Tu b'Shvat, the New Year for trees, came from biblical roots but was not celebrated as a festival until about the tenth century AD. It is the only later festival that I have given a chapter because of the positive biblical teaching that it provides. After that there was another very long gap until the twentieth century when two new memorial days were added to the Jewish calendar. Both are in the time between Passover and Pentecost. The first is Yom ha Shoah or Holocaust Memorial Day. This commemorates the six million Jewish people who were murdered in Nazi Europe between 1939 and 1945. It is appropriate to have this day in a mourning period in the calendar. The second occurs eight days later and is called Yom h'Atzmaut or Israel Independence Day. This celebrates Israel's declaration of independence on 14 May 1948, which was 5 Iyar in the Jewish calendar.[11] This completes the Hebrew calendar of the year.

A Feast of Seasons

I write this book out of the experience of spending the last ten years on the staff of the Church's Ministry among Jewish People (CMJ). For much of this time I lived in North London, where many of my friends were Jewish believers in Jesus who were particularly keen to keep all the festivals. Having grown up in the mainstream church, it has been an immense privilege to have lived and breathed the Jewish festival year as well as my own traditional Christian one. To those who have had this experience, the question that naturally arises is which should be the normative feasts for those who seek to follow Jesus in a New Testament context? In the final chapter I will consider whether Christians should regularly practise the Hebraic festivals or see them as something of historical and biblical interest alone. Here I shall also look at the Christian calendar and see how and if the two can fit together.

I would like to invite you to discover these biblical feasts and enjoy the richness of the seasons that await you.

Notes

1. Strassfeld, M., *The Jewish holidays, A Guide and Commentary* (Harper and Row: New York, 1985), p. 106.
2. The Rosh Hashanah tractate of the Talmud begins with a description of four New Years in Judaism.
3. Safrai, C., 'Jesus' Jewish Parents', *Jerusalem Perspective*, vol. 40 (Sept/Oct 1993), pp.10–11, 14–15.
4. Luke 2:23; Leviticus 12:8.
5. See for example Matthew 12:1–14.
6. See for example the Golden Rule of Matthew 7:12. Hillel was once asked to summarise the whole Torah while standing on one leg. He said, 'Whatever is hateful to you, do not do to others.'
7. Steinsaltz, A., *The Essential Talmud* (Basic Books, Inc: New York, 1976), p. 27.
8. 'Menahem the Essene', *Encyclopaedia Judaica CD ROM Edition,* Version 1.0 (Judaica Multimedia (Israel) Ltd; text: Keter Publishing house Ltd: Jerusalem, 1997).
9. 'Kabbalah', *Encyclopaedia Judaica CD ROM Edition*, Version 1.0 (Judaica Multimedia (Israel) Ltd; text: Keter Publishing house Ltd: Jerusalem, 1997).
10. In America the Reform and Liberal movements are known as Conservative and Reform respectively.
11. Problems with the two calendars became apparent in 1998 when 5 Iyar occurred on 30 April. Israel took some time to decide which date should be chosen for their fiftieth anniversary.

Chapter Two

PASSOVER – SACRIFICED FOR US

One of my clearest childhood memories is of a Last Supper meal at my primary school. It was approaching Easter and we had been deep into making cards with Easter eggs and rabbits. Then it was announced we were to have a Passover meal to learn about the Last Supper. We went into the assembly hall where rugs were laid out, picnic fashion. I can remember very little of the event except that it involved cheese biscuits and blackcurrant squash! There was something very special about it, however, and somehow it linked Jesus to Moses and the Last Supper to the Israelites. From that moment on, I had no doubt that the Old and New Testaments were fundamentally connected.

So what is Passover and why does it take on such a great significance for the followers of Jesus?

The origins of Passover

Passover is the oldest and greatest of the festivals. It begins on the eve of 14 Nissan in the Jewish calendar. This month is in the spring and marks the start of the festival year in the ancient biblical calendar, where it is called Aviv. Though it is a very old festival, its folk origins were probably in two even more ancient festivals which were celebrated by the ancestors of the Israelites.[1]

Nomadic spring festival

The pre-Israelite nomadic shepherds of the Middle East also held a festival in the spring. It was the month when the lambs gave birth, and the fourteenth and fifteenth day of a lunar month was the time of the full moon. A sheep or goat may have been sacrificed as a thanksgiving for the new birth of spring, and it is quite possible that this would have been the firstborn of the flock. This lamb would then be eaten by the family. It may be that the early Israelite shepherds also daubed the blood of their lamb on the tent posts of their tent as a protective symbol against plague and misfortune. Like Passover, it was a family festival, conducted at night by the head of the family.

Early agricultural festival

Passover is also known as the Feast of Unleavened Bread and in this respect rests on an ancient festival for settled farming communities. The two earliest grain crops to ripen in the Middle East are wheat and barley. Barley ripens first and tolerates drier conditions. Wheat grows in slightly wetter conditions and ripens about seven weeks later. The beginning of the barley harvest coincides with Passover whereas the start of the wheat harvest occurs at Pentecost.

Festival of deliverance

These may be the folk origins of the festival, but there is something else about Passover that lifts it above the traditional festivals of shepherds and farmers. The experiences in Egypt and the Exodus of the Israelites transformed this festival into a celebration of deliverance. The Exodus from Egypt is the foundational experience of the Jewish people. The Israelites' experience in the wilderness on their way to the Promised

Land changed them from a band of escaped slaves into a nation. Moreover, the experience of their miraculous escape from Egypt and their protection in the wilderness formed them into a covenant people that from that time onward looked to God as their focus and sovereign.

The key person associated with the Exodus is Moses. The book of Exodus begins with the story of the oppression of the Israelites under the Egyptians, and an account of Moses' birth and unusual childhood in the household of Pharaoh. Moses' privileged position gave him the ability to see the injustice his people were suffering, but did not give the skills and spiritual maturity needed to lead his people to freedom. That came after many years of exile in Midian, where he tended sheep and learnt to seek God. He doubtless learnt much from his father-in-law, Jethro, who also worshipped the God of the Hebrews. It was in the wilderness that Moses had his major experience of God who appeared to him in a burning bush, and commissioned him to lead his people to freedom:

> The Lord said, 'I have indeed seen the misery of my people in Egypt. I have heard them crying out because of their slave drivers, and I am concerned about their suffering . . . So now, go. I am sending you to Pharaoh to bring my people the Israelites out of Egypt.' (Exodus 3:7, 10)

Moses took some persuading that he was the right person for the post! In the end God also appointed Aaron, his more eloquent brother, to be his spokesperson. Together they returned to Egypt and began the tasks of first persuading the Israelites to follow their lead, and then convincing Pharaoh to let the Jewish people go. One of the most famous passages in the Exodus story concerns the plagues that God sent on the Egyptians to make them free the Israelites. In the Passover service these plagues are commemorated by dipping a finger into a full wine glass and dropping a drop of wine onto a plate while reciting the names of each of the ten plagues: blood; frogs; gnats; flies; pestilence; boils; hail; locusts; darkness; and slaying of the firstborn. To the modern Passover participants the drops of wine look very like drops of blood and remind them of their own suffering and of the suffering of the Egyptians.

Slaying of the firstborn

The Exodus begins with Passover. This part of the story centres on the final plague, the slaying of the firstborn, described in Exodus 12. Each household took a year-old lamb without defect, and on the fourteenth day of the month of Nissan, they slaughtered it at twilight. The blood was smeared on the tops and the sides of the doorframes and the meat was eaten that night with bitter herbs and unleavened bread. It was eaten in haste, with staff in hand and long clothing tucked into a belt (this is the meaning of the old biblical term, 'loins girded'). On that same night the Lord passed through Egypt slaying the firstborn of every household and every animal. Where the blood was on the doorposts, the Lord 'passed over' the home and the household was safe. This festival was also commanded to be a lasting ordinance, and to be celebrated annually throughout all generations.

The Israelites obeyed and it was exactly as Moses had said. Just as Pharaoh had killed all the boys of the Israelite families in Moses' childhood, so now the Egyptians woke to find their firstborn sons dead. Pharaoh summoned Moses and Aaron and commanded them to go, taking all their people and possessions with them. So they left, heading for the desert to avoid the heavily fortified coastal road. There follows the famous story of the parting of the sea (Exodus 14), and the stage is set for God to deal with his people during the forty years in the wilderness, before they finally entered the Promised Land. This is the biblical origin of the festival of Passover ('Pesach' in Hebrew), the name deriving from the action of the Lord in passing over the protected Hebrew homes.

Passover in Temple times

Once established in the land of Israel, Passover began to develop as a seven day national holiday. In the north it remained a local festival with lambs sacrificed on the high places and this tradition is still continued by the Samaritans on Mount Gerizim. For Judah in the south, once the Temple had been built, the Passover celebrations became centred on Jerusalem, as one of the three 'pilgrimage festivals'. Each of these had a harvest and an Exodus or wilderness theme.

There were several great Passovers recorded in the Old Testament. King Hezekiah celebrated Passover as part of his reforms (2 Chronicles 30). He was forced to celebrate it a month late because there were not enough priests consecrated by 14 Nissan, and there had not been time to assemble the people. When they did come to celebrate the festival they kept it for a double, fourteen day period, because there was so much rejoicing. Sadly this revival was not sustained after Hezekiah's death, but his great grandson, King Josiah, after discovering the law of the Lord, commanded that the Passover feast should be reinstituted (2 Kings 23:21–23). There was another long gap before finally, under Ezra, the exiles from Babylon observed the festival (Ezra 6:19).

Song of Songs

It is traditional to read the Song of Songs on the first Sabbath after the start of Passover. This beautiful love poem is set in the period between Passover and Pentecost.[2] Each of the plants described in the book is in flower at this time or has fruit. The rose of Sharon and the lily of the valley, the walnut and the pomegranates are in bloom, and the mandrakes are producing their fruit, which is the only time when they have a sweet fragrance.[3] This gives us a very vivid picture of spring in Israel and the rich landscapes through which the pilgrims would have travelled. In Judaism, the interval between Passover and Pentecost is a period of waiting. This links beautifully to the hope and fulfilment theme of the lovers who are betrothed and looking towards their marriage union. Traditionally weddings are not held in the period after Passover, but at Pentecost.[4]

Passover in New Testament times

As I explained in Chapter 1, Jesus came from a particularly devout Jewish family, and probably went up to Jerusalem for Passover every year of his life (Luke 2:41). The population of the city at that time would have been about 100,000. At Passover this would have more than doubled. It was the custom for people to open their homes to visitors but not to accept payment. Instead, the skins of the sacrificed animals would usually be given to them.[5] Jesus would undoubtedly have had many friends and possibly relatives in the city, with whom he would have stayed. For Jewish people living beyond Israel, the journey up to Jerusalem may have been a rare, or even a once in a lifetime, experience. These pilgrims would be less likely to know people in Jerusalem. Many would still find accommodation amongst the hospitable Judeans, and others would come with tents that they would erect outside the city walls. These pilgrims were Jews and converts to Judaism from all over the ancient world. Some would primarily come as merchants with things to sell over the holiday. The Roman Procurator would journey up from Caesarea and be quartered at Herod's Palace. There would be extra Roman troops as this was a key time when they feared that a revolt would break out.

The permanent residents of Jerusalem had spent many days or weeks preparing their homes. They had to be swept out, prepared for all the visitors and in particular cleaned of all leaven. Anything that had yeast within it had to be removed from the house. On the morning before Passover the final scrap of leaven from every home was burnt. The head of the house would have had to procure a Paschal lamb. These had to be year-old males without defect. Perhaps a relative from the country might bring one or more lambs with them, which would then need to be taken to the Temple to confirm their suitability. Alternatively, a Paschal lamb might have been purchased from the Temple. On the day before the festival, at midday, the lambs were taken to the Temple to sacrifice. The owner of the lamb himself killed the animal while the priests sang the Hallel. This comprised Psalms 113–118 and Psalm 136 and was also sung on Pentecost and at the Feast of Tabernacles. The Talmud describes the priests as wearing scarlet robes and holding basins of gold and silver. When a sacrifice was made, the nearest priest would catch the blood. This was passed back along the row to be poured out at the base of the altar. The men returned with their slain lambs and in the evening would roast them in clay stoves that stood in the courtyards of their homes. All the family would dress in white festive garments. Those leading a Passover Seder still sometimes wear a Kittel, or white ceremonial garment.

For many, the cost of a Paschal lamb was beyond them. Households would come together and share a lamb between them. There was a minimum amount of lamb that you had to eat to say that you had taken part in the Passover, but this was only the size of an olive. This meant that one Paschal lamb could be used for a very large number of people, but it would not be sufficient for the meal itself. For this reason other lambs could be slaughtered as additional food for the meal. These would be considerably cheaper than the Paschal lamb, and did not have to be totally consumed on Passover night. Presumably large amounts of extra meat would have been needed for an extended Passover family gathering.

The Passover Seder

It is impossible to reconstruct exactly what happened in a first-century Passover celebration. We can look at the oldest Jewish sources, however, and gain a few clues about the Passover nights that would have been experienced by Jesus throughout his life.

Hillel, the famous rabbi of Jesus' childhood, said that there were three things that were essential to a Passover celebration. These were the Paschal lamb, unleavened bread (matzah) and bitter herbs. He suggested that these were eaten ('bound') together, making a kind of sandwich. It is thought that this might have been the method used to eat the very small piece of Paschal lamb. Each of these things was to remind the descendants of those who came out of Egypt of what God had done for Israel. The lamb would remind them that God had passed over their homes; the unleavened bread would remind Israel that God had redeemed them; and the bitter herbs would remind them of the bitterness of slavery under the Egyptians.

It became traditional for the leader of the Passover to give this sandwich, as a special privilege, to someone on whom he wanted to confer a blessing and show his regard. We cannot be certain if this tradition was established in Jesus' day, but it is thought by some to be the origins of the sop given to Judas.[6] If this were the case it would reveal the deep unconditional love of Jesus even to the one whom he knew would betray him.

By the first century, it had become traditional for the youngest son to ask four questions at the Passover. He would begin by asking why this night was different from all other nights. Then he would ask why on this night the family ate unleavened bread, bitter herbs, dipped their food twice and ate the special Paschal lamb. After the destruction of the Temple, the question about the Paschal lamb was changed to ask about reclining to eat. The Romans reclined to eat their banquets and this became the custom for wealthier Jewish people. The rabbis declared that all Jews should recline for the Passover since all should celebrate freedom on that night. This may have been practised in Jesus' day, since we know that Jesus 'reclined at table' on that night (Luke 22:14). These four questions are still a central part of the modern Passover.

In a modern Passover there are four cups of wine to drink, two before the meal and two after the meal. These are to remember the events of Exodus 6:6–7: I will bring you out; I will free you; I will redeem you; and I will take you as my people. In the time of Jesus we cannot be clear that this tradition had already begun, though two cups of wine would have certainly been drunk as they were traditional in all Jewish ceremonial meals. In the Passover ceremony, a piece of unleavened bread is broken and hidden at the start of the meal. This is known as the afikomen. It is found and eaten at the end of the meal, just before the Redemption cup is drunk. This piece of hidden bread has been linked to the Messiah. Many Christians believe it was the afikomen and the Redemption cup that were taken by Jesus to institute the Lord's Supper.

At the end of the Passover meal, the participants would remain and sing the Hallel Psalms. Many would make their way to the Temple where they would pray until late into the night in the hope and expectation that the Messiah would come. In the account of the Last Supper the disciples first sang a hymn before going up to the Mount of Olives. This was probably the Hallel. Jesus asked them to pray with him into the night.

The First Fruits

On the second morning of Passover, the priests would go out to the Kidron Valley and cut the first sheaf of the newly ripened barley harvest. This was brought in to the Temple and presented as a wave offering. If we follow the timetable of

John's Gospel, this first fruits offering was being presented at the Temple early on Easter Sunday morning and would have coincided with the resurrection of Jesus as first fruits from the grave.

What is a wave offering?

A wave offering is an offering to the Lord, which is later given as a gift to the Temple priests. It is believed that in Temple times, wave offerings were placed on both hands, held high and then the person offering the gift would rock forwards and back. The gift was thus presented to the Lord, but symbolically given back to the people. It may be that the traditional Jewish rocking, or davening, during prayer goes back to wave offerings.

Fixing the date

There is little doubt that the Last Supper contains elements of a Passover meal. But there is great debate as to whether it was celebrated on the actual night of Passover. The date apparently differs in the Gospels. Matthew, Mark and Luke place the Last Supper on the first night of Passover itself. This would involve the lambs being sacrificed on the afternoon before. There is a difficulty with this because it would mean that the following day was a Sabbath. Could Jesus have been crucified on that day? John has the Last Supper 'just before the Passover feast' (John 13:1), meaning the night before the Day of Preparation. Later John says that Jesus died on the Day of Preparation and that the next day was a special Sabbath (John 19:31). This timetable is supported by Jewish tradition, but it poses the problem that Jesus could not have had a Passover meal.

How do we draw these two traditions together? It is possible that there could have been more than one calendar operating. For example, the Sadducees and Pharisees had different methods of calculating Pentecost, so they may have disagreed on the date of Passover. The Synoptic Gospels (Matthew, Mark and Luke) might have followed the Pharisees, who were closest to Jesus' own tradition. John may have been the disciple who 'knew the High Priest' (John 18:15), and used the calendar of the Sadducees. This would make it possible to have had the crucifixion on the Pharisees' first day of the feast, which was the Sadducees' eve of Pesach. However, there is no firm evidence that Passover was kept on different days by the Pharisees and Sadducees.

An Essene home?

In recent decades the idea that Jesus celebrated Passover in an Essene home has been proposed. They may also have taken another calendar. Although their main centre was at Qumran, they also had houses in Jerusalem. The traditional location of the upper room is in the Essene area of the upper city. Interestingly, they were an all-male community, and so it would be likely that a man would carry a water jar, a task normally undertaken by women (Mark 14:13). In Jewish ceremonial meals, such as Shabbat, the blessing is said over the wine first and then the bread. In the Essene community this order was reversed.[7] This could be evidence for an Essene link to the Last Supper and Christian Communion, though the use of the afikomen followed by the Redemption cup would also produce an order of bread followed by wine.

Jesus ate in the homes of tax collectors and publicans, though he did not agree with their ideology.[8] If the Essenes did have a different calendar, it is not impossible that Jesus might have taken advantage of an Essene contact to be able to celebrate a Passover meal on the night before he died, even though it was one night early. John mentioned the date but the other Gospel writers did not. By this timetable Jesus would have died as the Paschal lambs were sacrificed and would have risen from the dead on the morning when the first fruits were being offered at the Temple.

A Jewish Christian theory

Alfred Edersheim was a Jewish believer in Jesus in the nineteenth century and, like many of the Jewish Christians of his day, he had extensive rabbinical knowledge. He pointed out that there was a second offering which could have also been called the Passover.[9] On the first night families ate the Passover lamb which had been sacrificed on that day, but this was not the only lamb to be offered. On the next day a festive offering called a 'Hagigah' was sacrificed, as a peace offering. Edersheim suggests that these were the lambs being offered at the Temple at the time of Jesus' death. The Passover lamb was roasted and eaten with unleavened bread and bitter herbs. But the Hagigah was boiled and eaten alone. John states that the priests did not want to enter Pilate's house because they would have been ceremonially unclean and could not have eaten the Passover (John 18:28). It would have been permissible to eat the Passover lamb because someone else could have offered it on their behalf. By the evening when it was time to eat the sacrifice they would have become clean again. But they could not have eaten the Hagigah because this must have been both sacrificed and eaten in ritual purity. The Hagigah is at times referred to as the Passover sacrifice in the Old Testament, so John could also have referred to it in this way.

Using this timetable, the Passover lambs were killed on 14 Nissan, which was Thursday afternoon. On the start of the 15th Jesus ate the Passover with his disciples (Thursday evening). Later on the 15th (Friday during the day) he hung on the cross at the same time as the Hagigah or peace offering lambs were being sacrificed. Edersheim did not consider that the priestly authorities would try to prevent the Romans executing people on that day, and Jesus could have been buried because it is permitted to bury people on festivals as well as the Sabbath. On the morning of the 16th, the first sheaf of the harvest was cut and offered as the first fruits offering. On the Sunday morning of the 17th, Jesus rose from the dead as the first fruits from the grave.

Edersheim's theory is the neatest of those concerning the exact timing of the Last Supper, though this will always remain an enigma. I believe that it is more important to establish that it coincided with the Passover season than to be able to calculate exactly the days when each event happened.

From Passover to Easter

The question many Christians ask is how did Passover develop into the Easter tradition? Some Christians believe it was purely to distinguish the Christian festival from the Jewish one. Others are more positive and see the natural development of an independent tradition. In reality, it was probably a combination of both motivations. No record is left of how the resurrection was celebrated in the very early years of the church and the first accounts that we have are from the second century AD. By then there were two traditions.[10] Some Christians kept very closely to the Passover roots and celebrated Easter on the first night of Passover, that is 14 Nissan, and for this reason they were called the 'Quartodecimans' meaning the 'fourteeners'. They placed the emphasis on Jesus as the Passover lamb, which is also the central theme of John's Gospel. These Christians largely lived in Asia Minor. The second tradition was to celebrate Easter on the Sunday after Passover. This was a main tradition of the church in Rome and these Christians placed an emphasis on the resurrection of Jesus on the first day of the week. The Quartodecimans also followed the Jewish practice of having a fast before Passover. In the Jewish tradition this led up to the Passover meal, but Christians fasted and prayed throughout that night and broke their fast with Communion at about three in the morning. This prayer paralleled Jewish prayer and praise after the Passover meal in the expectation that the Messiah might come.

From the middle of the second century onwards, the Roman Church tried to enforce its calendar for Easter. The date was finally decided at the Council of Nicaea in AD 325. Easter was to be celebrated on the first Sunday after the full moon that directly followed the Vernal Equinox (21 March). In most years this would coincide with Passover, but it would not always be so. The Eastern Churches still retained the earlier Passover practice for several centuries, and the British (Celtic) Church did not adopt the Roman calendar until Roman missionaries arrived in the sixth century.

From Last Supper to Eucharist

It is also important to consider how the elements of the Passover meal developed into Christian Eucharist or Holy Communion. The first Communion after the resurrection was presided over by Jesus himself at Emmaus (Luke 24:13–35). This would still have been within the eight days of Passover and so unleavened bread would have been provided for the meal. It was only when Jesus said the blessing and broke the bread that the disciples recognised him.

We might expect that Communion would have only been celebrated annually on the eve of Passover. However, it is clear from the New Testament that the believers remembered the death of Jesus through bread and wine as a regular part of their common life. The descriptions are generally in the context of an actual meal and Communion was seen as a foretaste of the heavenly messianic banquet.[11]

During the first hundred years of the church the meal associated with Communion disappeared. We do not know why this happened, although 1 Corinthians 11:17–22 gives some clues. As many non-Jews came into the church, the spirituality of Communion as part of a meal may have been lost. Paul advises Christians to eat in their own homes before coming together for the Lord's Supper, and that advice may have become the tradition of the whole church.

Justin Martyr wrote one of the earliest complete accounts of Communion after the New Testament. Breaking of bread was described in the context of a service and occurred every Sunday. The service followed a synagogue pattern of reading from scripture, a sermon, prayer, and then the Eucharist was presided over by the leader of the congregation. The term Eucharist was used and its meaning 'thanksgiving' was the central theme of the celebration.[12]

For the early Christian community, the Passover context of Communion very quickly developed into a regular community meal context. This gradually became established on the first day of the week and, within a hundred years, the meal faded out, leaving Communion to be the centre of a thanksgiving service.

Passover through the ages

In the third century, among the teaching written down for the first time in the Mishnah was all the instructions concerning Passover and the verbal order ('Seder' in Hebrew) for the ceremony on Passover night. Much of this reflected the traditions that were current in New Testament times. By the Middle Ages the Seder had developed in different communities into elaborate liturgies based on material from the Bible, the Mishnah and other sources. Known as a Haggadah, each liturgy book would also contain songs and would often be elaborately decorated.

There were significant changes once the Temple disappeared. The festivals began to be based around the home. For Passover the emphasis was no longer on obtaining and sacrificing a Paschal lamb, but on keeping the Passover Feast in families. Some families, especially in the Middle East, continued to eat roasted lamb, though they would not make a sacrifice. For many Jews, the inability to have a Passover lamb meant that this was the only meat they did not eat on this night. Instead there were two symbols, a lamb bone and a roasted egg. These were added to the traditional foods of bitter herbs, unleavened bread or matzah, four cups of wine, and a dip called clay or haroset, which was a sweet mixture and was introduced to lessen the bitterness of the herbs. It was mandatory to recline, and the Seder contained four questions from the youngest son, which would prompt the telling of the Passover story by the adults. This passing on of the remembrance of God's redemption of the Jews from Egypt continued to be the key theme.

A time to fear

From the Middle Ages onward, Passover was a particularly fearful time for Jewish communities in Christian lands. The Crusaders may have precipitated this. As they marched through Europe towards the Holy Land to fight the Muslims, they saw the Jews in their own countries as the 'infidel in their midst'. At Easter and Passover feelings were particularly sensitive and Christians accused their Jewish neighbours of being Christ-killers and ultimately of the crime of deicide, or of killing God. Good Friday was always a vulnerable day when itinerant preachers might take this as a theme for their sermons. In the twelfth century a new twist was added which became known as the Blood Libel. It was a charge that Jewish people killed Christian children for primitive rites. There began to be a terrible fear whenever a child went missing, because the Jews in the community would inevitably be blamed and would suffer. Though the church authorities investigated and repudiated the allegations, they still remained a strong part of European folk superstition. This might seem understandable in the context of the Middle Ages, but there were still instances in the twentieth century and the Blood Libel became part of Nazi propaganda.

In fifteenth-century Spain many Jewish people had reason to fear the Inquisition. This was the background to a very strange prayer that comes at the end of the Passover meal, and asks God to pour out his anger on the nations who do not recognise him. An outer door was traditionally opened at this point to allow the prophet Elijah to enter. The Messiah was expected at Passover and would be preceded by the prophet Elijah. The door was left ajar to symbolise the hope that Elijah would come and herald the Messiah. In many communities in Spain and elsewhere this was highly dangerous, as there might have been enemies outside. The prayer was for protection from these attackers.

Persecution is so much a part of Jewish history that it is impossible to consider many of the festivals without considering its impact. This racism against the Jews culminated with the Nazi Holocaust and many Haggadahs of the twentieth century have extra prayers added to commemorate those who were murdered.

Next year in Jerusalem

When the Temple was first destroyed and the Jews found themselves in exile, a new prayer was added to the end of the Seder, and this was prayed in hope for 2,000 years. It was the words, 'L'shana habaa b'Yerushalyim' or 'Next year in Jerusalem'. Through all those years of fear and precarious living in lands dominated by other peoples, there was the hope that God really would restore them to the land of Israel and that they might again celebrate Passover in freedom. Though there always were Jewish people in the Holy Land throughout the last 2,000 years of history, they were a minority. The main populations were in Tiberias and Safed in Galilee, and also in Jerusalem. In the nineteenth century a new movement started in Europe, when secular Jews began to get a vision for returning to the Holy Land. They bought up land, and started collective farms or kibbutzim. Christians who were sympathetic to Jewish people also shared this vision. Men such as William Wilberforce, Charles Simeon and Lord Shaftesbury all believed that the Jews would return to the Holy Land. This view was inspired by the belief that the return of the Jewish people to the land of Israel and their discovery of Jesus as their Messiah would be linked to Christ's Second Coming. This return has developed from an idealistic vision to the reality of the present State of Israel and today, during Passover, Jerusalem is once again full of pilgrims coming up to celebrate the feast.

A modern Passover Seder

A modern Orthodox Jewish family will prepare for Passover for weeks ahead. The house has to be totally spring-cleaned to make sure that absolutely no leaven is left. Passover crockery for both meat and milk meals are brought out. Any cooking pots that are used during the rest of the year have to be made kosher for Passover by placing under a flame. Special foods are prepared and arrangements made for large family gatherings.

On the first night, the table is set with the Passover dinner service. There are two candles for the mother of the house to light, and the matzah (unleavened bread) is placed in a special cover. The other ceremonial foods are arranged on an ornate plate, which also holds the shank bone of the lamb. Wine glasses are on the table and sometimes an ornate cup for the father. There is always an extra place laid for Elijah and he has an extra large cup filled to the brim.

The candles are lit, the family gathers and the Seder begins. As they go through the ancient rite, there is a sense that they too were once slaves in Egypt and God also brought them out from there. The food, when it finally arrives, is the best meal of the entire year and at times everyone reclines (or at least leans, with their left elbows on the table) to remember the old tradition. The ceremony is a long one and there are many extra bits for the children to keep them awake, including some special nonsense songs at the very end. Finally, in the early hours of the morning the Seder ends and the children are gathered up and taken off to bed. There are still seven more days of Passover, when only unleavened food is eaten and sometimes families have a second night Passover Seder, either in another family home or, especially among Reform Jews, in the synagogue itself.

A Messianic Seder

Having been to a number of Seders in the homes of Messianic friends, on one Passover I decided to hold one in my own home. I chose second night, when the family Seders had passed, and invited a number of friends, most of whom were Jewish. I had been 'on the road' doing Passover demonstrations for a couple of weeks beforehand. I love this time of year, and, however often I present the Passover Seder, it is always fresh. By this point in the season, however, there is one bit that makes me smile. When it comes to the part 'Why is this night different from all other nights', I mentally alter the words 'different from' to 'the same as'! Two of my guests were in similar positions and so we decided to keep things brief and mainly concentrate on the Passover songs and sung parts of the liturgy that are too complex to present in churches. Every time we came to a bit with a famous melody someone at the table would start it off. The only snag was that my guests represented many different traditions from Orthodox to Liberal. Everyone seemed to start on the same note but then take off in two or three different directions. Inevitably we discussed which was the 'right' tune, and inevitably nobody could agree! It was a humorous evening and helped me to understand the diversity of Jewish tradition. Sometimes, at the end of a Passover demonstration, I am asked about something in my presentation that differed from another Passover demonstration. I remember my Messianic Passover with its musical debates and explain that there are so many traditions for Passover, that most things are authentic for somebody's community somewhere in the world.

Making the link

Passover and Easter are inextricably linked, and understanding the Passover traditions will greatly enhance Christian understanding of the death and resurrection of Jesus as well as the Last Supper account. In the intervening centuries, Passover and Easter have developed different traditions and responded to different conditions. It is particularly important to understand the history of persecution that Jewish people have experienced at Passover time if we are to understand the significance of having a 'Christian Passover'. This could not have taken place a few hundred years ago or even a few decades ago in some European countries.

It is also important for Christians to understand Passover for its own sake. Jewish people see the Passover and Exodus as the formative period for them as a people. In the Old Testament itself this is the pivot around which all of the rest of the teaching and history rotate.

Youth track

Design a drama based on the Exodus story. Try to keep it fairly short and find out if it could be used in your congregation over Easter. Your youth group may also like to try a Passover Seder as the climax to your spring programme.

Your own Passover Seder

Your Passover may be anything from a simple supper to an elaborate meal. Either is suitable, as at different times of their history Jewish people would have experienced both. I have included a short Haggadah for you to use at your Passover Seder. It follows the ancient order of a Jewish Passover, but I have also included New Testament references to help you make the link to the Last Supper. This should be read at the meal table, with part of it coming before the meal and part after. You can choose your readers for different parts.[13]

Participants

There needs to be a main father and mother. The mother's role is to light the candles and say a prayer. The father's part is the largest and can be shared, especially if you are not in a family group. There also needs to be a youngest child who has a small part to read. There are six short passages from the Bible and these can be shared around the table.

Setting the Table

Your table should have:

A white tablecloth
Two candlesticks with white candles and matches
A matzah cover containing three pieces of matzah
A large white napkin
A Seder plate with the ceremonial food
Red wine or grape juice
A small bowl of salt water
A small plate and a glass for each person, for the ceremonial part of the Seder
A large bowl and a jug of water with a towel near the table.

A Seder plate can easily be made out of a large platter or else a round tray. This needs to be small enough to fit on your table but large enough easily to fit five small bowls in a circle. These bowls are each filled with a different ceremonial food: haroset, horseradish, parsley, a roasted egg and lettuce. There should also be room to fit a lamb bone among your circle of dishes.

Making a matzah cover

These are usually circular and made of four pieces of fabric sewn on top of each other. You can make it out of cotton, silk or a synthetic fabric, and it will usually be white. If you are able to find wide material (over 48 in, 120 cm wide) you may be able to cut four circles all in one row and so will only need 12 in (30 cm) of fabric in total.

You will need:

Four circular pieces of white fabric 12 in (30 cm) in diameter
36 in (90 cm) decorative braid about ⅝ in (1.5 cm) wide
40 in (1 m) lace or an edging designed to fit around a circle about 1½ in (3 cm) width
Cotton threads in white, a colour to match your braid, and one to match your lace.

Edge each of your circles with a zigzag stitch on a sewing machine to prevent them from fraying. If you do not have a machine, edge by hand using blanket stitch.

Choose one to be the top piece and draw out a Star of David on the middle of it. Each side of the star should be about 5 in (12 cm) long. Cut a 16 in (38 cm) length of braid and fold under ½ in (1 cm) at each end and sew to stop the braid fraying. Place the braid along the marks of one half of the star (this should trace out the shape of a triangle). You will need to fold it carefully at the first two corners and make sure the ends will join up at the third corner.

Pin and tack in place and sew firmly by hand or with a machine. Repeat for the other triangle of the star using the other piece of braid. Next, place your lace trim around the edge of the circle of cloth. Cut to length and finish the edges as with the braid and then pin and tack around the circle. Sew firmly in place.

You are now ready to assemble your matzah cover. Place the circles of cloth on top of each other with the decorated circle on top. Join around the edge with pins. It is important to leave a gap big enough to easily fit pieces of matzah into your cover. You may like to use a piece of matzah to measure this, or mark about one third of the circumference not to be sewn and tack around the other two thirds. Remove the pins and sew carefully around the two thirds of the circumference, making sure that you join all four circles together.

Your matzah cover is ready for use. You should have three

pockets – place a piece of matzah in each and set on the table.

Ceremonial food for Passover

How to make haroset

1 apple, grated
1 teaspoon cinnamon
2 tablespoons sweet red wine or grape juice
1 tablespoon chopped walnuts
1 teaspoon honey

Prepare all the ingredients and then mix together well. The resulting mixture should be lumpy and of a similar consistency to heavy porridge or moist stuffing. If you have a food processor, the easiest way to make haroset is to blend it all roughly in one go, adding the apple at the end. The proportions are not exact but are based on a family meal for six to eight people.

Roasted egg

The easiest way to create a roasted egg effect is to boil an egg and then light a match under it when it is cool.

Parsley and lettuce

Have enough so that each person can have a couple of pieces each.

Horseradish

Freshly grated horseradish is most authentic but very hot. It is traditional to grate it together with cooked beetroot and this lessens the intensity. Horseradish sauce is more easily available and is perfectly acceptable.

Lamb bone

This should be a shank bone. Roast a leg of lamb in the weeks coming up to Passover. After your meal, boil the remaining meat off the bone and then leave it in the bottom of your oven for a few weeks to totally dry it off. This should remove all of the meat, although I did once have a dog run off with one! If a real bone is impractical or you are a vegetarian, make one out of cardboard or modelling clay.

Matzah

This should be available in most supermarkets. It is the modern unleavened bread that is more like a large biscuit. Sometimes they are in boxes that say 'Not Kosher for Passover'. There are subtle differences but, unless you are in a Jewish home using special Passover crockery and a kosher kitchen, your Passover will not be technically kosher anyway, so these matzahs are fine. There are fourteen in an average box. You will only need about half a piece per person. Place three in the matzah cover and any others on a plate on the table. It is important that they are not broken beforehand.

Red wine or grape juice

There are four 'cups', so about one bottle is needed for every six people. Each 'cup' needs only be enough for a toast to be drunk.

A Passover menu

If you want to approximate a kosher meal there are certain details to remember. No flour, bread or raising agent can be used in any part of the meal. If meat makes up part of the meal, milk, cream or other dairy products must not be used in any part of the meal. No pork or seafood should ever be used. Do think through how the meal will be served. It will not be easy to do much last minute preparation just before you serve (this is where slow cookers and heated trolleys come into their own!). The most solemn part of Passover Seder comes immediately after the meal, so leave the clearing up until the end of the evening.

To start

Boiled eggs served with salad

Main course suggestions

Chicken in orange sauce
Baked potatoes
Green vegetables

Dessert suggestions

Cinnamon balls and coconut pyramids

Recipes

Chicken in orange sauce[14]

This is an Israeli-style dish and is very good for Passover, as it will keep in a moderate oven for a long time, while you are having the first part of your Seder. If you use a slow cooker, follow the manufacturer's instructions for chicken casseroles.

For 6 people

6 chicken portions
1 large onion, chopped
1 clove of garlic, crushed
Olive oil
2 tablespoons matzah meal (or potato flour)
Salt

¾ pt (430 ml) orange juice
1 teaspoon cinnamon
4 cloves
2 oz (55 g) almonds (optional)
3 oz (85 g) raisins

Using a frying pan, sauté the onions and seal the chicken pieces in the oil and garlic. Place into a casserole dish or slow cooker. Add the matzah meal, salt, cinnamon and cloves to the fat in the pan and stir to a smooth paste. Add the orange juice slowly, stirring all the time. Bring mixture to the boil and pour over the chicken. Cook at a moderate temperature, 160°C (325°F, gas mark 3) for two hours or until the chicken is cooked. It can remain in the oven for another hour while you have the first part of your Passover Seder.

Cinnamon balls

Cinnamon balls and coconut pyramids are Ashkenazi Passover recipes, popular among British Jews.

2 large egg whites
2 tablespoons sugar
1 tablespoon ground cinnamon
8 oz (225 g) finely ground almonds
1 tablespoon potato starch

Grease two large baking sheets, then coat them with extra potato starch, tapping off excess. Beat egg whites until foamy, and then beat in the sugar. Continue beating for several minutes until the whites form stiff shiny peaks. Stir in the almonds, cinnamon and potato starch until well combined. Form into small balls and place about 2 inches apart on the sheets. Bake for 15 to 20 minutes in a moderate oven 160°C

(325°F, gas mark 3). They should be firm and lightly browned. Store in airtight container.

Coconut pyramids

These are symbolic of the pyramids the Israelites were made to build.

2 egg whites
6 oz (170 g) desiccated coconut
3 oz (85 g) caster sugar
1 tablespoon potato starch

Prepare tins as for cinnamon balls. Whisk egg whites stiffly. Add sugar and continue beating until the whites form stiff shiny peaks. Stir in coconut and potato starch and mix well. Form into pyramids and arrange on tins. Bake in a very moderate oven (140 °C, 290 °F, gas mark 2) for 20 minutes or until they are slightly golden on the surface.

A Haggadah for believers in Jesus

Lighting the festival candles

Mother Blessed are you, O Lord our God, King of the Universe, who has sanctified us by your commandments and commanded us to kindle the festival lights.

The first cup – I will bring you out

All glasses are filled, but we do not drink yet. For each cup it is traditional to lean on one elbow.

Father Blessed are you, O Lord our God, King of the Universe, creator of the fruit of the vine. Let us give thanks for this Passover feast, which commemorates the departure from Egypt and freedom of the children of Israel from slavery. Blessed are you, O Lord our God, King of the Universe, who has kept us alive, sustained us and enabled us to reach this season.

All drink from the first cup.

Reading 1: Luke 22:14–16

Washing of hands

Only the father washes his hands at this point. He should hold his hands over the bowl and another participant should pour water over them.

Ritual dipping of parsley

Father As we take this parsley and dip it into the salted water let us remember the tears of the Hebrews in bondage; and let us remember the suffering of Jesus on our behalf. We dare not take for granted what God has done for us. Let us remember the hyssop that was dipped in the lamb's blood for wiping on the doorposts and lintels; and let us remember Jesus' blood shed for us. Let tears of repentance never be far from us.[15]

Each person takes a piece of parsley and dips it in salt water.

Father Blessed are you, O Lord our God, King of the Universe, creator of the fruit of the earth.

Everyone eats parsley.

Reading 2: Exodus 6:6–7

Breaking the middle piece of matzah

The father takes the middle piece and breaks it in two. One half is put back between the other two pieces, while the other half is wrapped in a napkin and placed to one side. This second half, now called the afikomen, is hidden.

Father This is the bread of affliction which our ancestors ate in the land of Egypt; let all those who are hungry enter and eat thereof and all who are in want come and celebrate the Passover. At present we celebrate it here, but next year we hope to celebrate it in the land of Israel. This year we are servants here, but next year we hope to be free in the land of Israel.

Telling the story

All glasses are filled a second time, but we do not drink yet. First, the children ask their questions. There are several parts for children in the Passover Seder, reflecting their different personalities. There is a wise son, a wicked son, a simple son and one who is too young to ask a question. The most important is the youngest son who asks the question 'Why?' The adults then recount the story of the Exodus, so passing on the story to the next generation.

Youngest child Why is this night different from all other nights? On all other nights we may eat leavened or unleavened bread, but on this night why do we only eat unleavened bread? On all other nights we may eat any kind of herbs, but on this night why only bitter herbs? On all other nights we do not dip even once, but on this night why twice? On all other nights we eat and drink either sitting or leaning, but on this night why do we all lean?

All Why? To remember that we were all slaves of Pharaoh in Egypt and that if the Lord had not brought our fathers out, they and we and all our children would still be there in bondage.

Reading 3: Exodus 12:1–14

Father Our own hard hearts can separate us from God's rich blessings – though not from his love – if we refuse to submit to him in love and obedience. The Lord comes in judgement on people, as he did on Pharaoh and the Egyptians.[16]

As we remember the ten plagues, for each plague mentioned we dip a finger into our wine and spill that drop of wine on our plates. Why? Because even the suffering of our enemies pains us. God himself is grieved at the wickedness of, and therefore the need for judgement on, those who oppose him.

All These are the ten plagues that God brought on the Egyptians: blood, frogs, gnats, flies, pestilence, boils, hail, locusts, darkness, slaying of the firstborn.

At this point Psalms 113 and 114 would be recited to a traditional melody. Either read from these Psalms or choose a suitable song that you are familiar with.

The second cup – I will set you free.

Lift your glass with your right hand and lean on your left elbow.

Father Blessed are you, O Lord our God, King of the Universe, creator of the fruit of the vine.

All drink the second cup.

Ritual washing before food

It is traditional for the father of the household to wash the hands of his family by pouring water over their wrists and palms.

Reading 4: John 13:1, 4–5

Father Blessed are you, O Lord our God, King of the Universe, who has sanctified us with your commandments and commanded us to wash hands.

The father washes the hands of the others.

The next section concerns the three essential elements of Passover.

A blessing for daily bread and unleavened bread.

The father takes the matzah and holds it high.

Father Blessed are you, O Lord our God, King of the Universe, who has sanctified us with your commandments and commanded us to eat unleavened bread. Blessed are you, O Lord our God, King of the Universe, who brings forth bread from the earth.

A small piece of matzah is eaten from the top and the middle piece.

Bitter herbs

The father takes pieces of bitter herbs and dips them in the haroset. He gives them to each person, though they are not eaten yet.

Father Blessed are you, O Lord our God, King of the Universe, who has sanctified us with your commandments and commanded us to eat bitter herbs.

All eat bitter herbs.

Binding – the sandwich

Father Rabbi Hillel took the unleavened bread and bitter herbs and ate them together with the Paschal lamb that he might perform what is said, 'With unleavened bread and with bitter herbs shall they eat it.'

Each person should take two pieces of matzah and put bitter herbs between them to make a sandwich, which they eat.

The meal

Father Let us eat together the eggs to begin our meal. In this way we celebrate the feast of life. And then let us enjoy our meal.

The meal is now served.

Towards the end of the meal the children are asked to go and search for the afikomen, the piece of matzah which was hidden. The adults may like to have a present for the one who finds it.

Grace after the meal

Father When you have eaten and are satisfied, praise the Lord our God (Deuteronomy 8:10).

The third cup – I will redeem you.

All glasses are filled but do not drink yet.

Father Traditionally this cup is known as the 'Cup of Redemption'. We move into this part of the Seder aware that at about this stage Jesus began to move into the deepest mystery of all. He must have shocked his disciples with his interpretation of this third cup and the afikomen. Let us move forward with him.[17]

Reading 5: Corinthians 11:23–26

Father Let us eat together from the matzah, which was hidden, the last piece of the meal to be eaten. Blessed are you, O Lord our God, King of the Universe who gives us Jesus to be the bread of life.

Everyone eats a small piece of matzah.

Father Blessed are you, O Lord our God, King of the Universe, who gives us Jesus to be the true vine.

All drink the third cup.

Traditionally Psalms 115–118 and 136 would now be sung. This would be an appropriate time for prayer and worship.

Elijah cup

An extra cup is now filled to overflowing for the prophet Elijah and a place has been set for him. The door is left ajar so that he can enter the room easily.

The children can search for Elijah.

The fourth cup – I will take you as my people

All glasses are filled, but do not drink yet.

Father This is known as the cup of completion. Passover ends with the words 'Next year in Jerusalem'. May our greater hope be that Jesus will return to Jerusalem and reveal himself to his people, Israel.

Blessed are you, O Lord our God, King of the Universe, Creator of the fruit of the vine.

All drink the fourth cup.

Father Accomplished is the Passover Service according to its laws and statutes. Let us end with words from scripture.

Reading 6: Hebrews 13:20–21

All Next year in Jerusalem!

Notes

1. Schauss, H., *The Jewish Festivals* (Jewish Chronicle Publications: London, 1986), pp. 38ff.
2. Song of Songs 2:11.
3. Song of Songs 2:1, 6:11, and 7:13 respectively.
4. Neot Kedumim, *The Biblical Landscape Reserve in Israel*, Trail A (Neot Kedumim: Israel, 1992), pp. 27–33.
5. Schauss, H., *op cit*, pp. 48ff.
6. Edersheim, A., *Jesus the Messiah* (Longman, Green and Company: London, 1889; reprinted: Wm. B. Eerdmans Publishing Company: Grand Rapids, MI, 1979), p. 550.
7. Flusser, D., *Jesus* (The Magnes Press: The Hebrew University, Jerusalem, 1998).

8. See for example Luke 19:1–10.
9. Edersheim, A., *op cit*.
10. Bradshaw, P., *Early Christian Worship* (SPCK: London, 1996), pp. 80ff.
11. Acts 2:42–47 and 1 Corinthians 11:17–34.
12. Chadwick, H., *The Early Church* (Penguin: London, 1967), p. 261.
13. I am particularly grateful to my former colleagues, Margaret Heron, who produced a Haggadah on which this present one is based, and Walter Riggans, who allowed me to use some prayers from his Haggadah.
14. I am grateful to another former colleague, Ursula Jones, for these Passover recipes.
15. Riggans, W., *In every generation, a Seder for believers in Yeshua* (All Nations Christian College: Ware, 1987), p. 7A.
16. *ibid* p.10A.
17. *ibid* p.16A.

Chapter Three

PENTECOST – FIRST FRUITS OF THE HARVEST

Have you ever been reading a book and found the drama so exciting that you have been tempted to sneak a look at the final page before you get to it?[1] Sometimes books keep us in so much suspense that the temptation to read ahead is almost irresistible. Most Christians, if asked about the origins of Pentecost in the Bible, would direct the enquirer to Acts 2 for the description of the pouring out of the Holy Spirit on the first followers of Jesus. In this tremendous story we have not the origins of Pentecost but its final climax in the Bible. When we skip to the last page of a book, we get the answers but do not always understand them because we have missed the build up of the plot. In a similar way, when we start at Acts 2, we find the results of Pentecost but miss much of the meaning in the events. What is the background to the feast of Pentecost in the Hebrew Bible?

The origins of Pentecost

To discover the origins of this festival, we need to turn to the time when God's people, the Israelites, were in the desert at

Mount Sinai (Exodus 19–34). Here the Shekinah or Glory of the Lord descended in fire on the mountain. Moses went up to meet with the Lord and God confirmed his covenant with his Israelite people. Moses recorded God's teaching, the Torah, for his people. The rabbis believe that the whole of the Pentateuch (the first five books of the Bible) was given to Moses at this time. In the account in Exodus we find a selection of the teaching recorded which includes the Ten Commandments and various social laws. In Exodus 23:14–19, the three annual festivals were established: the Feast of Unleavened Bread (see Chapter 2), the Feast of First Fruits, and the Feast of Ingathering (see Chapter 6). The second of these, First Fruits, is the festival that we know today as the feast of Pentecost.

Giving the first fruits

In Leviticus 23:9–21, two first fruits festivals are explained. The first was for barley offered at Passover. This barley sheaf was called the 'omer' and began a period of counting for fifty days, during which time the barley crop was harvested. This period was known as 'counting the omer' and by the fiftieth day the wheat was ripe. The very first to ripen was harvested, baked into two loaves and offered to the Lord as a wave offering. This is the second first fruits festival mentioned in Leviticus 23 (verses 15–21) and is the feast of Pentecost.

Names for the festival

'Pentecost' is the Greek name and relates to the fifty days from Passover. 'Shavuot' is the Hebrew name and this literally means 'sevens' or 'weeks' and refers to the seven weeks counted after Passover. In biblical times it was also known as 'Yom ha Bikkurim', meaning 'Day of the First Fruits' (Numbers 28:26), 'Hag ha Kazir', meaning 'The Harvest Feast' (Exodus 23:16), and 'Atzaret', meaning 'The Closing'. This last title refers to its role as the end of the Passover feast.

Pentecost in Temple times

Pentecost was the second of the three pilgrimage festivals and it was especially important for farmers to come up to Jerusalem and offer the first fruits of the wheat harvest, baked into two loaves. Between Pentecost and Tabernacles, the first fruits of other crops were brought up.

There were many rules governing these first fruits. Some rabbis considered that all crops should be brought, others thought that only the seven species in Deuteronomy 8:8 should qualify. These were barley, wheat, grapes, figs, pomegranates, olives and dates. They could only be brought by legitimate owners of land in Israel. They had to be carried personally and given to the priests by the owner. It was said that the king himself had to carry his offering on his own shoulder. When the offering was given to the priest, the giver would make a declaration, which is recorded in Deuteronomy 26:

> My father was a wandering Aramean. He went down into Egypt and lived there and became a great nation. But the Egyptians ill-treated us and made us suffer. So the Lord brought us out of Egypt with a mighty hand and an outstretched arm. He gave us this land, flowing with milk and honey: and now I bring the first fruit of the soil that you, O Lord, have given me. (Deuteronomy 26:5–11, abridged)

The first fruits could be brought in at any time between Pentecost and Tabernacles. After Tabernacles they could still be brought but the declaration could not be said. Those who lived close to the Temple brought fresh fruit, and those who lived far away brought dried fruit.

Bikkurim procession

In the Talmud there is a moving description of farmers bringing in the first fruits or Bikkurim. People in a local area assembled with their first fruit offerings in a basket. It was said that rich people would cover their baskets with gold and silver but poorer people would have plain baskets of wicker or willow. Special decorative fruits were placed on the top of the baskets to make them look attractive, even if the actual first fruits were dried. Two pigeons or turtle doves were tied to the baskets to be offered at the Temple. The farmers would then go up together to the city of Jerusalem, carrying their baskets on their shoulders. They would have an ox at the front of their procession which would have horns covered in gold and a crown of olive branches on his head. Flutes were played and Psalms 122–134 were sung as the procession went up to the city. When they arrived, priests from the Temple met them, singing psalms and with great rejoicing. The pilgrims would enter the Temple and hand over their baskets as they recited the declaration from Deuteronomy 26.

The feast of Shavuot and the Bikkurim are placed together in both the Bible and the Talmud, so one could suppose that they might have occurred at the same time. However, all fruit had to be fully ripe before they could be brought to the Temple. Since only barley and wheat are ripe by Pentecost, it is not clear whether the complete first fruits ceremony happened during this festival or later in the year.

A festival with no date

Another uncertainty is the actual date for Pentecost in the Jewish calendar. The Bible counts the days from the barley offering at Passover:

> From the day after the Sabbath, the day you brought the (barley) sheaf of the wave offering, count seven full weeks. Count off fifty days, up to the day after the seventh Sabbath, and then present an offering of new grain to the Lord. (Leviticus 23:15–16)

During the time of the Second Temple, there was division over the meaning of this text. The Sadducees maintained that the Sabbath mentioned in this verse was the first Saturday after the beginning of Passover. This would mean that Pentecost would always fall on a Sunday, seven weeks after Passover. The Pharisees considered that the Sabbath referred to was the first day of Passover, on whichever day of the week it fell. The counting should therefore begin on the second day of Passover and Pentecost would occur on the fiftieth day after Passover, which is 6 Sivan in the Jewish calendar.

If we follow John's account of the death and resurrection of Jesus, the first day of Passover was on a Saturday. This would make the two dates of Pentecost coincide for that year. The Pharisees' date has been passed down as the modern date for Shavuot in Judaism.

The Holy Spirit in the Hebrew Bible

> In the beginning God created the heavens and the earth. Now the earth was formless and empty, darkness was over the surface of the deep, and the Spirit of God was hovering over the waters. (Genesis 1:1–2)

The Spirit of God is central to the Bible and is introduced in the very first verses of the Hebrew scriptures. In the beginning of the world the Spirit is involved in creation. He directs the forces of nature and keeps the human world in check (Genesis 6:3; 8:1). In Hebrew the word used is 'ruach' which literally means 'wind' or 'breath'. From Genesis 2:7 we find that the breath (ruach) of life was breathed into Adam to make him alive and is therefore necessary for life. Psalm 104:29–30 states:

> When you take away their breath,
> they die and return to dust.
> When you send your Spirit,
> they are created.

This life-giving Spirit is also mentioned in the famous passage about the dry bones in Ezekiel 37. Ezekiel is commanded to prophesy to the bones, so that breath will enter them and they will have life. Ezekiel prophesies and the bones come together – tendons, flesh and skin cover them but there is no breath (ruach) in them. As Ezekiel prophesies again, the breath enters them and they become a living army – the whole house of Israel. One purpose of this vision was to show that the Spirit gives not only natural life but also spiritual life to God's people.

Resting upon and indwelling

The Spirit of the Lord is seen dwelling in people such as Joseph (Genesis 41:38), and coming upon people, such as Samson (Judges 14:19). When the Spirit came upon people they experienced God's supernatural power and were sometimes able to do extraordinary feats, such as when Samson tore a lion apart with his bare hands (Judges 14:5). This coming upon people could happen in a variety of situations and was a temporary event in the Old Testament. The indwelling was reserved for exceptional people of God including Joshua (Numbers 27:18), David (Psalm 51:10–11), and Ezekiel (Ezekiel 3:24). The term 'anointing' is also used to describe this deeper indwelling of the Spirit. Isaiah 61 refers to an anointed prophet of the Lord, or the Messiah, and Jesus quotes this at Nazareth. Joel 2:28 states: 'I will pour out my Spirit on all people.' This is quoted in Acts 2 at Pentecost and indicates that the indwelling of the Spirit is no longer restricted to a few exceptional people, but the disciples of Jesus will all experience the deeper indwelling of the Holy Spirit.

The Holy Spirit

The term Holy Spirit (Ruach haKodesh) is only mentioned three times in the Hebrew Bible. In Psalm 51:11, David appeals to God 'Do not cast me from your presence, or take your Holy Spirit from me.' In Isaiah (63:10–11), it is in the context of Israel's rebellion against God. The Israelites are described as having the Holy Spirit among them in their journey through the wilderness, but are now charged with grieving the Holy Spirit. It is clear from this that the Holy Spirit is the same person as the Spirit of God and the Spirit of the Lord mentioned elsewhere in the Hebrew Scriptures.

The Shekinah

The Glory of the Lord ('Shekinah' in Hebrew) also describes the Holy Spirit in the Old Testament and is manifest by fire. The Lord led his people through the wilderness with fire, and, when the covenant was confirmed with the Israelites at Mount Sinai, God descended on the mountain in fire (Exodus 13:21; 19:16–17). When the first Temple was dedicated to the Lord and the Ark of the Covenant was placed in the Holy of Holies, the Shekinah of the Lord came and filled the Temple. Similarly, when Isaiah had his vision of the Lord at the start of his ministry, smoke filled the Temple as the Shekinah came down (Isaiah 6:4). We find no mention of the Shekinah filling the Temple when it was rebuilt after the exile, and Haggai talks about the 'former glory' of the Temple (Haggai 2:3). We cannot assume that the Shekinah never came to the Second Temple simply because it is not mentioned in the Bible but, given that there is also no account in the rabbinic literature, it is possible that the Shekinah did not return after the destruction of the original Temple. There was still the hope that the Shekinah would come, and, later in Haggai, we find the promise that 'the glory of the present house will be greater than the glory of the former house' (Haggai 2:9).

All these different aspects of the Spirit's personality are woven together in the Hebrew Bible and create a picture of God's Spirit, which was recognised by the disciples when they received the Holy Spirit at Pentecost.

Pentecost in Later Judaism

After the destruction of the Temple in AD 70, it was no longer possible to bring in the first fruits of the wheat harvest to the Temple and a new meaning had to be given to this festival if it was not to fade away. Already there had been a search for this among the urban populations of the Diaspora who had no first fruits to bring. Groups such as the Essenes were also looking for less agricultural meanings. They found it in terms of the renewal of God's covenant with Noah and God's promise to all humanity.

The giving of the law

The Pharisees also linked Pentecost to God's covenant but they turned to Mount Sinai. They calculated that, since Moses met with God and received the Torah fifty days after Passover, this would have been on Shavuot. Thus Shavuot in post-Temple Judaism became a celebration of God giving the law at Mount Sinai.

In medieval times Jewish children would start to learn Hebrew on Shavuot. As they studied they were given cakes or sweets, so that the Torah would be sweet to their lips. Some would even find the letters coated with honey, so as they learnt the sound of each one they could lick away the honey![2] It became traditional to study the Torah all night before the festival. Various reasons are given for this, including the legend that when Moses came down the mountain he found all the Israelites asleep. Staying up all night ensures that you are awake to receive God's word when it is given.

Israel's wedding

Jewish weddings always have a ketubah. This is a special marriage document, which states the obligations of a husband to his wife. Sephardi Jews have a custom of drawing up a ketubah on Shavuot. The people of Israel represent the groom, and the bride is the Torah. During the Shavuot service at the synagogue, this ketubah is read out. It includes the words, 'I betroth you to me for time everlasting and I betroth you to me with faithfulness . . . My desire is for the Holy Torah to be my bride and for her to be inscribed on my heart.'

Akdamut

Messianic hope is not absent in post-Temple Shavuot. Another Shavuot text, associated with Jewish communities from Eastern Europe, is the Akdamut. This was written in the eleventh century by Rabbi Meir ben Isaac Nehori. It is an imaginative poem which describes the creation of the world, the giving of the Torah to Israel, Israel's faithfulness through great trials and a journey to the golden thrones of heaven when Israel is finally redeemed. The Messiah awaits them under a canopy of light and the messianic banquet has been prepared. This poem is traditionally recited with Exodus 19, which is the Torah portion for the festival.[3]

Modern customs

In modern Reform Judaism, Shavuot was chosen as the day to have confirmation services for boys and girls, replacing the traditional Bar Mitzvah, which occurred on the first Sabbath after a boy's thirteenth birthday. 'Bar Mitzvah' means 'Son of the Commandment' and is the time when a young person takes on the responsibility for keeping the law or Torah.

In Israel today the first fruits aspect of Shavuot has been revived. Children wearing hairbands of flowers, and carrying baskets of fruit and flowers, make a procession to the synagogue. There is much singing and dancing, and tambourines, recorders and other instruments may be played in the procession. Homes and synagogues are decked with greenery and flowers as a reminder of spring. There is a legend that Mount Sinai itself was green and covered with flowers, even roses, when God gave the law to Moses.

It is traditional to eat dairy foods on Shavuot. There are a number of legends concerning this. The Torah is compared to milk, because it contains everything needed for nourishment, just as milk is a complete food for a baby. Milk is the food of the spring, after the young animals have been born. A more exotic legend is that the Israelites had been fasting while Moses met with God. After Moses came down the mountain with the law, the Israelites were so hungry that they could not wait to kill and prepare meat, so instead made a meal of dairy food. Whatever the reason, dairy foods such as cheese blintzes and cheesecake are strongly associated with this festival.

Ruth and King David

The book of Ruth is traditionally read during Shavuot. It is a beautiful story of the devotion of a Moabite girl, Ruth, to her Hebrew mother-in-law, Naomi, and through her to the Lord, the God of the Hebrews. Ruth's commitment to Naomi, and her own piety, led Naomi's relative, Boaz, to marry her and become the kinsman redeemer to the family. This was the closest relative who provided security for the family and in some cases became father to an heir. Ruth and Boaz had a son, Obed. Through Obed, Ruth became the ancestor of King David. There are a number of reasons given to explain why Ruth has a place in the festival of Pentecost:

1. The story of the book takes place during the barley harvest, that is during the weeks between Passover and Pentecost. As a spring harvest story it is very fitting to place it with the festival of first fruits.
2. In Jewish tradition, King David has a special association with Pentecost. Since Ruth is the ancestor of David, it is fitting to remember her for this reason.
3. Ruth converted to Judaism and so became part of the covenant people of God. Pentecost is a celebration of the

giving of the law and the giving of the covenant to the Jewish people.
4. Ruth's loyalty to Naomi and to the Lord is symbolic of Israel's loyalty to the Torah.

For Gentile Christians, Ruth's story also reminds us that, through her descendant Jesus, God has grafted us into his covenant people.

In memory of a king

King David has a particular relationship with this festival, since tradition states that he was born and died on this day. David was the greatest of the Israelite kings. He came from Bethlehem, the place that Ruth adopted as her own, and his childhood was spent as a shepherd boy in the hills around the town. He rescued his people by means of a smooth pebble and a simple sling and went on to become a wise and great leader. God made a covenant with David and promised that from his seed would come the Messiah. It was King David who first planned to build a Temple for the Lord, a plan that was brought to fruition by his son, King Solomon. On the second night of Shavuot, after all the festivities of the day, a memorial candle is lit in Orthodox synagogues and people gather to recite the Psalms of David in memory of his death.

Pentecost in the New Testament

The Gospels record that Jesus went up to Jerusalem for Passover and Tabernacles but there is no mention of Jesus worshipping at the Temple during Pentecost. This does not necessarily mean that he never visited the city at this time, but it does reflect the lesser significance of this festival compared to the other two pilgrim festivals. It mainly had significance for those who had crops with first fruits to bring in and had less meaning for town inhabitants. During Jesus' three years of ministry, he spent this season in the Galilee region. It was after the rains but before the really hot weather and hence an ideal time for itinerant teaching.

Although the festival of Pentecost was left out of the Gospel accounts, this is amply made up for in the book of Acts. After his resurrection, Jesus appeared to his disciples for forty days. This was during the counting of the omer. Before ascending into heaven he left specific instructions that his followers were not to leave Jerusalem until they had received the gift of the Holy Spirit (Acts 1:1–5). In his Gospel account, Luke records that they stayed continually at the Temple, praising God (Luke 24:53).

Upper room or Temple?

The image many Christians have of the disciples at this point is of a frightened band of men and women praying together in an upper room. This was the position of the disciples before Jesus appeared to them after his resurrection, and they returned to an upper room to choose a replacement for Judas.[4] Can we assume that they were in the same upper room when the Spirit came in Acts 2? There are arguments, which may indicate that they were, in fact, at the Temple:

1. This was the habitual place for prayer and worship. As mentioned above, after the ascension of Jesus, the disciples returned to the city and continually worshipped at the Temple (Luke 24:53).
2. Pentecost morning would be a natural time to go to the Temple, to be able to take part in the first fruit celebrations.
3. Acts 2:1 states that they were all together in one 'place'. This could be the upper room but it might be elsewhere.
4. The archaeological evidence of the city for this time indicates that, though it would have been possible to find a room to accommodate a hundred or so people, the streets

were narrow and it would have been difficult for large crowds to gather in them. Had the disciples been in the Temple courts, however, it would have been easy for a crowd to gather. Given that this was where the majority of the population was on Pentecost morning there would have been a crowd readily available.

These arguments indicate the possibility that the disciples were at the Temple. This must be balanced by the tradition that they were in the upper room. It is very probable that, wherever the disciples were when the Spirit came upon them, they did make their way to the Temple on that day. They were almost certainly there for the baptism of Jesus' new followers.

Where were the new believers baptised?

The logistics of the baptism of 3,000 new believers, described in Acts 2:41, puzzled practically-minded scholars until the southern wall of the Temple Mount started to be excavated in the 1970s. Archaeologists discovered large numbers of mikvot (ritual immersion pools) before the steps leading up to the Temple. It is clear that Jewish pilgrims would have immersed themselves on the way up to the Temple, so that they would have been ceremonially clean for worship.

Before this discovery, scholars had hypothesised that the new believers had water poured on them or even that they made the strenuous fifteen-mile hike to the River Jordan! The mikvot give a straightforward solution, as there were ample facilities to baptise several thousand believers in one day. One can only guess at the impact this would have made on the other pilgrims entering the Temple.[5]

God's holy fire

The Shekinah of the Hebrew Bible is a manifestation of the Holy Spirit in fire. It was this Shekinah that came down on the disciples praising God together in the Temple courts on

Pentecost morning. God's presence filled his house and God's new covenant people were filled with power to proclaim his message – 'The Messiah is risen – he is Jesus, Son of David.'

Making the link

We can now draw together the threads of Old Testament and Jewish Shavuot and apply them to New Testament Pentecost. We can see several themes emerge.

First fruits and harvest

In the minds of the disciples this festival would, first and foremost, be about first fruits. How appropriate that, on the very day that the first fruits of Israel's grain crop were being brought into the Temple in the form of freshly baked loaves, the first fruits of God's spiritual harvest were offering their lives to him through repentance and baptism.

Shekinah and covenant

The covenant with Moses was made at Pentecost and the Torah traditionally given to Israel at this time. God came in fire on Mount Sinai at Pentecost to seal his covenant with his people Israel. At New Testament Pentecost he came in fire again, this time to dwell in his people. A renewed covenant was sealed with the indwelling of the Holy Spirit and the law written on the hearts of all believers.

Waiting

The counting of the omer was traditionally a time of waiting. The first disciples of Jesus prayed and waited from his resurrection and ascension until the coming of the Spirit at Pentecost. This day marked the end of waiting and the time for proclamation!

Preparing for Pentecost

Decorate your home with flowers, greenery and possibly some wheat stalks. Bake some round challah bread, using the recipe in Chapter 10, and have a loaf with your meal at Pentecost to symbolise the first fruit harvest offering at Pentecost time. Pentecost is a festival of great celebration for Christians, because Jesus has sent us the Holy Spirit who has empowered us to proclaim his name. An open family meal could be an opportunity to include friends and neighbours. Why not invite them to join you?

Making a fruit of the Spirit tree

You will need:

A large dead branch
Adhesive or string
Pieces of stiff paper.

A good idea for children is to make a fruit of the Spirit tree. Talk about fruit: what is your favourite and what is it like?

Introduce the idea of the fruit of the Spirit (Galatians 5:22–23). Ask each child to draw their favourite fruit and write the name of one of the fruits of the Spirit on it. This can then be coloured, cut out and stuck or hung onto the tree.[6]

Youth track

All-night Pentecost pray-over

Have you ever stayed up all night to study the Bible? Well here is your opportunity to do so! In Jewish tradition, the Torah was given to Moses at Mount Sinai on the Feast of Shavuot. Because of this, many Jewish people will stay up to study the Bible all night on the eve of Pentecost. This is a challenge for Christians too. Here are some suggestions for a Pentecost study night. You might like to have the night entirely centred on Bible reading, or you may wish to include prayer and other activities. Some groups might like to use the event as an opportunity to raise awareness of and support for overseas mission. Below are a few ideas for structuring the night.

Begin the evening with worship followed by a light supper together some time around sundown. It is probably better to start around 9.00 to 10.00 pm rather than early evening. The two major activities I would suggest are Bible reading, for which there is a list of suggested passages below; and prayer, for which I would recommend selecting a few countries out of the book *Operation World*.[7] This gives a report about the church in each country and many pointers for prayer. You might also like to pray for mission partners you personally know, and your own church's overseas links.

Each hour could be divided as follows:

20 minutes Bible reading
10 minutes discussion
5 minutes introducing an area for prayer

20 minutes prayer
5 minutes break.

This will give you regular changes of activity. You might also include other activities such as showing a video, having games and quizzes, or having guest speakers to come and lead study sessions and times of worship. Activities which are interactive will be most effective as they will help keep people awake! In the breaks it is also important to have drinks available and possibly some light snacks. Towards daybreak, you could go to a suitable place to see the sunrise. It would be good to end with worship, followed by breakfast together.

Suggested passages are: Genesis 1–9; Genesis chapters 11–25:11; Exodus 1–3 and 13–14; Exodus 19–20 and 23:14–24:18; Exodus 32–34; Leviticus 23; 25; Ruth; Psalms 113–118; 136; one complete Gospel; and Acts. These sections have been divided as far as possible into twenty-minute sections, though some will be longer. The selection gives the covenant history of the Israelites, the key Old Testament passages on Pentecost, and the key New Testament passages.

Recipes

Cheese blintzes

Cheese blintzes are probably the most traditional of all Jewish dairy recipes for Pentecost. They can be eaten either as a main course with salad, or as a dessert.

For 10 blintzes

Batter

4 oz (110 g) flour
8 fl oz (220 ml) milk

2 eggs
¼ teaspoon salt
2 tablespoons melted butter
Butter or oil for frying
(For a sweet batter add 1 tablespoon sugar and 1 teaspoon vanilla)

Mix all the batter ingredients in a blender until completely smooth. Heat a non-stick frying pan over medium heat with some butter or oil. Drop just enough batter into the hot pan to cover the bottom well. Gently fry one side until edges are browned and the top is dry (1–2 minutes) – do not turn over in the pan. Set aside on a paper towel, cooked side upwards. Continue with remaining batter.

Cheese filling

1 lb (450 g) cottage cheese, or 1 lb cream cheese
½ teaspoon salt
1 tablespoon sugar
Butter for frying
(Add either 1 tablespoon of cinnamon or the grated rind of one lemon for flavoured fillings)

Mix all the ingredients together thoroughly. Place a heaped tablespoon of the mixture onto the cooked side of each of the pancakes. Wrap the sides of the circle over the filling to begin making an envelope. Then fold up from the bottom and the top. Set aside until the meal is to be eaten. Fry on both sides in butter until brown and crispy.

Cheesecake

(Grease a 9 in (23 cm) deep tin with a loose base)

For the base

8 oz (225 g) digestive biscuits, crushed
4 oz (110 g) butter or margarine

Melt the butter slowly in a saucepan and then add the biscuit crumbs. Spoon into the bottom of the tin and smooth down (a potato masher is quite good for this).

For the cheese filling

1½ lb (700 g) cream cheese or cottage cheese
7 oz (200 g) caster sugar
3 large eggs, beaten
Juice and rind of 3 small lemons
a few drops of vanilla essence

Combine all the ingredients (apart from the lemon and vanilla) in a food processor and beat until smooth (an electric beater could also be used). Stir in the lemon juice and rind. Pour into the tin. Cook in the centre of a cool to moderate oven, 170°C (325°F, gas mark 3) for 35 minutes. Cool in the oven for 1 hour. Store in the refrigerator.

Topping

The easiest topping is a tin of pie filling such as cherry or blackcurrant.

Variations: it is quite traditional to add sultanas to baked cheesecakes. For this, just use one lemon and add 4 oz (110 g) sultanas to the beaten cheese mixture. Serve the cheesecake plain or top with cream.

Notes

1. A version of this chapter was first published as: Hodson, M. R., *Pentecost Beginnings, a resource pack for churches and groups* (Olive Press: St Albans, 1998), and this contains further ideas for a church Pentecost celebration.
2. Black, N., *Celebration, The book of Jewish festivals* (Collins: London, 1987), p.140.
3. 'Akdamut Millin', *Encyclopaedia Judaica CD ROM Edition* Version 1.0 (Judaica Multimedia (Israel) Ltd; text: Keter Publishing house Ltd: Jerusalem, 1997).
4. Luke 24:33–36, Acts 1:12–26.
5. Notley, S., 'Discovering the Jerusalem of Jesus', *Bible Times*, vol. 1, no. 1 (1988).
6. I am grateful to CMJ member, Harry Johnson, for providing me with this idea.
7. Johnstone, P., *Operation World* (STL/WEC: Bromley, 1993 fifth edition). (This book is regularly updated, so look for the latest edition.)

Chapter Four

ROSH HASHANAH – A TRUMPET CALL INTO THE PRESENCE OF GOD

I have always loved the autumn. I think of it filled with cold, crisp, sunny days; of walks through golden woodlands, scrunching over the leaves; and of apple orchards waiting to be picked. Often it is the time for new beginnings. As a child, it would mean moving up to a new class with the challenges of new subjects and new friends to make. As an adult, it is still the time when new things begin, both at church and at work. For this reason it seems a more appropriate time for the year to begin, and so Jewish New Year, coming in the autumn, has a special place in my own personal calendar.

As I explained in Chapter 1, Judaism has four New Years, including one for festivals or cyclical time, and one for progressive or historical time. Rosh Hashanah is on 1 Tishri, which usually occurs in September and marks the start of the historical year. This is the beginning of the High Holy Days. The name 'Rosh Hashanah' means 'head of the year', indicating its importance as a New Year celebration. Its origins, however, are more to do with its role of starting and announcing the Days of Awe.

A feast of trumpets

Rosh Hashanah is first mentioned in the Bible in Leviticus 23:23–25, and it can also be found described in Numbers 29:1–6. The Israelites were commanded to gather for worship, do no work and hold a day for the blowing of trumpets. From this distance it seems a surprise to have a whole day devoted to trumpets. What was this all about? If we investigate trumpets in the Bible we will find that they have great significance for God and that this particularly fits in with this time of year.

There are several situations in which God commands a trumpet to be blown. They were to be sounded to remind the people to be obedient to God's command. In Numbers 10, for example, we find that Moses is commanded to make two silver trumpets for use when calling the community together and commanding them to break camp. The Jubilee Year was also announced by blowing the trumpet and began on Rosh Hashanah (Leviticus 25). Trumpets were to be used at festivals of rejoicing such as New Moon festivals. They were also to be sounded when going into battle, to ask for God's presence with his people. The classic example of this is Joshua at the city of Jericho.

The most important use of trumpets, however, is to announce a special presence of God among his people, and the most significant of all was when the trumpet was sounded to announce God's coming at Mount Sinai. Exodus 19 describes the event vividly. The Israelites were camped at the foot of the mountain. It was several weeks after they had left Egypt, and throughout that time they had been walking in the desert. Then they came to Mount Sinai, where Moses was commanded to ascend to meet with God. This was an incredible time, when the people turned to God as a community. They consecrated themselves for three days to be prepared for God to come among them. Only when the ram's horn had sounded were they allowed to approach the mountain. The Bible describes thunder and lightning and a thick cloud over the mountain. It then states that there was a loud trumpet blast causing everyone in the camp to tremble. It was in this way that God came down at Mount Sinai.

Trumpets were later spoken about in two other situations. King Saul used trumpets to try to guarantee God's blessing and affirm his own authority as king (1 Samuel 13). Saul desperately wanted God's presence with him, but he was outside God's will – even going directly against God's command. He therefore came under judgement. The second situation was a warning. In Ezekiel 33 we find that watchmen were commanded to blow a trumpet to alert people to danger. If the people took no notice, it was their own fault, but if the watchman failed to blow the trumpet and his neighbours were attacked, then he was accountable.

Trumpets are a wake-up call. When we hear the trumpet we must listen and take note. Most especially trumpets announce that we are about to come into God's presence. This is their importance at the start of the High Holy Days. We are about to go very specifically into God's presence and we need to take this time to examine ourselves and be prepared. Through the eight days following Rosh Hashanah, Jewish people take a dispassionate look at their lives and seek to put wrong things right.

A time to rejoice

It might be thought that Rosh Hashanah would be a solemn festival, but it is actually commanded to be a time to rejoice. The rabbis believe that this is to show our confidence in God's mercy:

> It is the custom for men, in front of a court of justice, to wear black and grow long beards as the outcome is uncertain. But Israel on Rosh Hashanah, wear white clothes, shave and eat, drink and rejoice in the conviction that God will perform miracles for them.[1]

We see this attitude demonstrated in the time of Ezra. It was the day of Rosh Hashanah when the Israelites assembled to hear Ezra read the Book of the Law. They had returned from long years of exile in Babylon and had forgotten both the Law and Hebrew, the language in which it was written. Nehemiah 8 describes the scene. Ezra stood on a specially constructed wooden platform and read the Bible from daybreak until noon. It is thought that the Levites translated the Hebrew Ezra read into Aramaic – the Babylonian language spoken by the returning Israelites. As the Israelites heard the Bible translated for them, they were filled with shame for not having kept the covenant with God, and began to mourn and weep. But Nehemiah commanded them to rejoice because the day was 'sacred to the Lord'. They were instructed to eat choice food and sweet drinks, and to send some to those who had none. This was to remember that the 'joy of the Lord is your strength' (Nehemiah 8:9–10).

Rosh Hashanah in later Judaism

Though Rosh Hashanah was not described as a New Year festival in the Bible, it took on this characteristic soon after the destruction of the Second Temple and certainly by the time the Mishnah was written in the third century. The two great themes of Rosh Hashanah are the creation of the world and the judgement of humankind.

King over creation

In the Talmud there is a debate over whether the world was created at Passover time or at Rosh Hashanah. In the end the rabbis decided that though the years of a king's reign were dated from Nissan, the month in which Passover falls, Rosh Hashanah is the anniversary of the creation of the world and this makes it the New Year of years. God as creator is celebrated as king over the world. He made the earth and he continues to sustain and renew his creation (see Chapter 8). Trumpets are used for proclaiming the entrance of a king and so it is a doubly appropriate theme for this season.

God's judgement

As God is celebrated as king over creation, so he judges his creation at this New Year time. This is partly based on Deuteronomy 11:12: 'the eyes of the Lord your God are continually on (Israel) from the beginning of the year to its end'. In other words, how you start your year will determine how it is ended. It is thought that there are three books: the book of life; the book of death; and an intermediate book. The rabbis believe that the very righteous go into the book of life, the very wicked go into the book of death and most of us end up in the intermediate section. The books are kept open until Yom Kippur. A person's behaviour during this time therefore seals their fate. This period is known as the Days of Awe and it is a period for self-examination. We need to put our lives in order to gain a place in the book of life, according to Jewish tradition.

Tashlich

In post-biblical times it became a custom to go to the nearest source of running water for repentance and prayer. The idea was based on Micah 7:19: 'You will again have compassion on us; you will tread our sins under foot and hurl our iniquities into the depths of the sea.' This and other verses are read and sometimes people turn their pockets out into the water, or throw pebbles or bread into it. There is much discussion over the origins of this ceremony, which may be pagan. Some of the rabbis believe that the significance of the running water is that it contains fish. Because fish never close their eyes, they symbolise the eyes of God from whom you cannot hide your sin.

Abraham and Isaac

One of the key biblical themes for Rosh Hashanah is the sacrifice of Isaac in Genesis 22. This is known in Judaism as the Akedah, which is the Hebrew word for binding. The binding of Isaac occurred on Mount Moriah, which is the traditional site of the Temple Mount. This gives a great significance to an event that for many Christians foreshadows the sacrifice of Jesus. Many Christians interpret the ram in the thicket, which became the substitute sacrifice, as Jesus. One reason for blowing the ram's horn on Rosh Hashanah is as a reminder of the ram, which was sacrificed instead of Isaac. The Akedah is seen as the ultimate personal sacrifice and obedience to God's will. Through the Akedah, we understand the commandment that everything must be given over to God. The philosopher, Philo, drew significance out of the meaning of Isaac's name, which is 'laughter'. He suggested that in the commandment to offer up Isaac, we can understand that God wants us to offer him our joy.[2]

One of the prayers for Remembrance at Rosh Hashanah refers to the Akedah:

> Remember, O Lord our God, your covenant with us, your kindness and the oath which you swore to Abraham our father on Mount Moriah. Consider our father Abraham who bound his son Isaac on the altar. He restrained his compassion in order to perform your will with a perfect heart. So may your compassion overrule your anger against us, in your great goodness, and may your great wrath turn aside from your people, your city, and your inheritance.[3]

In later Judaism, the sacrifice of Isaac was seen as an example of martyrdom. This was especially true during the Crusades, when many Jewish people would commit suicide rather than face massacre at the hands of the Crusader armies.

Rosh Hashanah and the New Testament

If we examine the Gospels from a Jewish perspective, we will see that Jesus was in the habit of going up to Jerusalem during the autumn festivals, though he may not have arrived by Rosh Hashanah. In John 10 we find that he took the decision not to go publicly in his final year and that his brothers challenged him on this. We shall examine this event more closely in Chapter 6 when we focus on the Feast of Tabernacles. Though there are no outright references to Rosh Hashanah in the New Testament, we do find that trumpets took on a symbolic significance in the early church and that this drew on the rich symbolism of the Old Testament tradition.

The watchman

Paul brought out the watchman theme in his first letter to the Corinthians. He considered the gift of prophecy and compared understandable prophecy to the clear sound of a trumpet. Paul declared that tongues without an interpretation are to be compared to not sounding a trumpet clearly: 'If the trumpet does not sound a clear call, who will get ready for battle?' (1Corinthians 14:8). The parallel to Ezekiel 33 is unmistakable. Rabbis of Paul's day did not need to give an exact Bible reference and explanation in their teaching. They knew that their Jewish listeners would be so steeped in the Bible – actually knowing it by heart – that just one or two words would take them straight to a whole set of ideas in the Hebrew Bible. Here, those reading Paul's letter would have been immediately transported to Ezekiel 33 and the responsibility of the watchman to give a clear call to those around him. Paul believed his churches to be accountable to God for clear teaching and he believed that those with the gift of prophecy had an imperative laid on them to use this gift in the building up of the church. Rosh Hashanah is the start of the High Holy Days and a period of self-examination and challenge. The prophet's task is to challenge the church, so that through examining our lives we will respond to God's call to live as his covenant people.

The return of Jesus

There are also references to trumpets in the New Testament associated with the last days and the return of Jesus. The first reference is in Matthew 24 where Jesus himself is describing the signs of the end of the age to his disciples. The first part of the chapter deals with the terrifying events of this time, building up to a crescendo in the return of 'the Son of Man'. It is here that trumpets are described:

> At that time the sign of the Son of Man will appear in the sky, and all the nations of the earth will mourn. They will see the Son of Man coming on the clouds of the sky, with power and great glory. And he will send his angels with a loud trumpet call, and they will gather his elect from the four winds, from one end of the heavens to the other. (Matthew 24:30–31)

Again, we must ask what Jesus' Jewish followers would have been thinking of in the imagery of the Hebrew Bible. Is there an event there that this would remind them of? It is clearly the culminating moment of history, the dramatic coming of God amongst his people. The most likely Hebrew Bible image would have been the Israelites at Mount Sinai. The clouds, the bright light of the glory, and of course the trumpets, would have brought Sinai images before Jesus' listeners. Sinai was the time when God confirmed his covenant with his people and made them his own. But there was another side to things: the terrifying holiness of God, the need for deep repentance and the need to be watchful for him. Jewish tradition states that when Moses finally came down the mountain, the Israelites had been waiting so long that they had fallen asleep. The second part of Matthew 24 is a warning to be alert and ready for Jesus to return at any time.

Paul used the same imagery when he spoke of the last days: in 1 Corinthians 15:52 and 1 Thessalonians 4:16 he describes the trumpet call that announces the return of the Lord and the raising of the dead in Christ. This will be the most momentous event in history and it would have been fitting to have seen it foreshadowed by the great Sinai event of Israel's history.

Finally, in Revelation, the symbolism of trumpets is used in announcing God's will, in announcing God's judgement and in announcing God's reign on this earth: 'The seventh angel sounded his trumpet, and there were loud voices in heaven, which said: '"The kingdom of the world has become the kingdom of our Lord and of his Messiah, and he will reign for ever and ever"' (Revelation 11:15).[4]

The imagery of the return of Jesus in the New Testament is interwoven with the imagery of trumpets, drawn from the Hebrew scriptures and through that the themes of Rosh Hashanah. We have a wake-up call, there is judgement and the trumpets are sounded to announce the return of the Saviour of the world.

Creation groaning

The two great Rosh Hashanah themes of creation and judgement come together in the New Testament in the book of Romans. In 8:18–25, Paul speaks about 'creation groaning' as it awaits redemption. Paul argues that human wrongdoing (original sin) has frustrated creation. We, as part of the natural world, are also experiencing that tension of being part of a marred creation. But we have a future hope of redemption and eternal life. Once again this places an eschatological slant on the links between this festival period and the New Testament.

Making the link

Four themes are interwoven at Rosh Hashanah: kingship and the idea that God is sovereign over all creation; remembrance and the belief that God judges our deeds; the coming of God amongst his people; and the final redemption in the future. If we compare these themes with the New Testament we find ourselves considering the return of Jesus and the final judgement. God continues to watch over his creation and, one day, Jesus will return as King Messiah to judge the living and the dead. Only then will there be final redemption and a kingdom which will have no end.

The tone of Rosh Hashanah then is a serious one, but also one of great joy as we look forward to the return of our Messiah in the future.

Celebrate New Year

This is a great festival to mark the start of the New Year for school-children. It should be a fun time, when we look towards the coming year and think of all the good things we would like to do and see happen. One of the traditions in Judaism is to eat slices of apple dipped in honey. This is to represent the sweetness of the year to come. Also make it a time to assess things and put things right. Maybe, to prepare for Rosh Hashanah, a bedroom tidiness competition would be in order with a honey muffin as a prize. (My husband has similar ideas for my study!) What things can we clear out at the start of the year both in physical ways and also in our own lives? Who should we write a card to when we have not been in touch for ages? Just like the secular year, Rosh Hashanah is full of good deeds and new resolutions.

Making New Year cards

It is traditional to send cards on Rosh Hashanah. These have a suitable picture on the front, like a ram's horn. Inside there is a traditional greeting such as 'Shana Tova', which means 'Have a

Good Year'. New Year cards are easily made from card or stiff paper. Great designs can be made using coloured paper, which can be stuck on the card to make a suitable picture.

Youth track

Looking to the future

Make a plan for the year ahead. What would you like to achieve? You might want to set goals for school work or sport. Maybe this is the year you might try to read the Bible right through! How would you go about this? (You can find ideas to help you in your local Christian bookshop.) Are there other things this year that you would like to plan for? Maybe you could help your grandparents, maybe improve your friendships or work on relationships that are difficult. What are your hopes and dreams? Find an exercise book and keep a weekly diary as the year unfolds.

Food for the festival

Challah loaves are traditionally baked in a round shape for Rosh Hashanah. Some traditions say that this is because it symbolises a crown and so reminds us that God is king over creation; other traditions say that it symbolises the blessings that will come to us all year round. Challah loaves often have raisins in them and are eaten dipped in honey even on the Sabbath, but not in salt, which is traditional for the Sabbath at other times of the year. Use the challah recipe in Chapter 10 and experiment by adding raisins. Honey is added to many of the savoury dishes to represent the sweetness of the year that we hope will come. Sweet fruits are also eaten and it is traditional to save an unusual fruit to eat on Rosh Hashanah. Apples dipped in honey are the most traditional fruit to be eaten, and this usually starts the main Rosh Hashanah meal.

Main courses might include fish cooked with honey, spices and raisins. A recipe for this is included in Chapter 5. Tzimmes, a dish made of carrots, prunes, and other vegetables in a sweet sauce, is an Eastern European favourite and surprisingly delicious. Because slices of carrots look like coins, it is hoped that this dish will symbolise prosperity in the coming year!

Honey cake is very traditional for Rosh Hashanah and everyone has their prize recipe. Mine is honey muffins, which are made with walnuts. If you do not have a muffin tin, the mixture will also be suitable for about eighteen 'English sized' small cakes.

Tzimmes

This is my version of a famous Ashkenazi Jewish recipe, which combines sweet and savoury ingredients. It lends itself well to a slow cooker and is great for a crisp autumn day.

For 4 people

1 lb (450 g) diced lamb or beef
4–8 small onions, halved or quartered
1 large clove of garlic
3–4 carrots, sliced into chunks (*Amounts of root vegetables can vary, but carrots are essential*)
1 parsnip, sliced into chunks
4–5 potatoes, sliced into chunks
10 stoned prunes
½ pt (300 ml) orange juice
½ lemon, sliced
1 teaspoon cinnamon
2 large teaspoons honey
3 cloves
1 stock cube (or a dessertspoon onion gravy mix)
Olive or other cooking oil

Heat the oil in a large pan. Brown the meat and sauté the onions and garlic. Transfer to a large casserole dish. Heat the orange juice and add the lemon and cinnamon, honey and stock cube or gravy mix. Add the vegetables and warm slightly. Transfer all the ingredients to the casserole dish and cook at 180°C (350°F, gas mark 4) for three hours, or until all the ingredients are cooked through. Serve with white cabbage, lightly cooked with caraway seeds.

Honey Muffins

For 12 muffins

3½ oz (100 g) butter
3½ fl oz (90 ml) strong black coffee
7 oz (200 g) honey
3½ oz (100 g) soft brown sugar
2 eggs, beaten

12 oz (340 g) self-raising flour
2 teaspoons lemon zest (optional)
2 teaspoons cinnamon
2 teaspoons mixed spice
2 teaspoons ground ginger
1 teaspoon bicarbonate of soda
2 teaspoons baking powder
3 oz (85 g) chopped walnuts

Line a 12-cup muffin tin with paper cups. Sift the dry ingredients (minus walnuts and lemon zest) together in one bowl. In a second bowl, beat together the sugar and butter until it is light and fluffy. Beat in the eggs adding some of the flour, if necessary, to prevent curdling. Fold in the dry ingredients alternating with the coffee and honey. (I usually find that alternating wet and dry ingredients is the best method of producing a light and well combined mixture). Finally fold in the walnuts and lemon zest.

Spoon into the muffin cases and cook in a preheated oven 200°C (400°F, gas mark 6) for 25 minutes.

Notes

1. Jerusalem Talmud, Rosh Hashanah 1:3,57 b.
2. 'Akedah', *Encyclopaedia Judaica CD ROM Edition Version 1.0* (Judaica Multimedia (Israel) Ltd; text: Keter Publishing house Ltd: Jerusalem, 1997).
3. Based on Singer, S., *The Authorised Daily Prayer Book of the United Hebrew Congregations of the British Commonwealth of Nations* (Eyre and Spottiswoode Publishers: London, 1962), p. 342.
4. See also Revelation 1:10; 4:1; 10:7.

Chapter Five

YOM KIPPUR – A TIME TO PRAY

It was Yom Kippur and six of us gathered in a flat in Hampstead. All of my friends were Jewish believers in Jesus and we had come together to commemorate this most solemn day in the Jewish calendar. Nine days previously we had experienced the joyous festival of Rosh Hashanah, and, in five days' time, we would celebrate Sukkot; but this was Yom Kippur and today we would fast from both food and water. We spent the day reading (and vigorously discussing) the traditional passages for Yom Kippur from the Torah and the Prophets, including the book of Jonah. We prayed, we examined ourselves, and we took a hard look at our little fellowship of Messianic believers. As we discussed the Hebrew Bible, it caused us to look at the New Testament and Jesus' death on our behalf. We ended the day with Communion, followed by light refreshments. As we parted, each was aware that we had gained a special bond through experiencing this day together.

The origins of Yom Kippur

In the wilderness

'Yom Kippur' literally means 'Day of Covering', that is, 'Day of Atonement'. As with many of the other festivals, we find the first mention of Yom Kippur in the accounts of the Israelites in the wilderness. While they were on their journey from Egypt to the Promised Land, God commanded that they make a Tabernacle for worship and sacrifices (Exodus 25). This would be a place where he would dwell amongst his people and meet with them. It would be a holy place where the community would see and experience God's glory. The centre of the Tabernacle was divided in two. The outer part was the Holy Place and here was a seven-branched candlestick called the Menorah, a table for the weekly offering of loaves, called shewbread, and a place for burning incense. The inner sanctuary was the Holy of Holies, where the Ark of the Covenant was kept. Inside the Ark was Aaron's budded staff, some manna and the two tablets of stone containing the law, which Moses had received on Mount Sinai.

Once a year, Aaron would enter the Holy of Holies to offer sacrifices for atonement.[1] He was to make a sacrifice first for himself, then for the Levites or priests and finally for the rest of the people. This was to be on the tenth day of the seventh month, which is nine days after the feast of Trumpets. He had to bathe, put on special garments and make sacrifices according to a prescribed order.

The High Priest

The Talmud gives a full description of the day as it was practised in the period of the Temple. A week before Yom Kippur, the High Priest would move from his own home in the upper part of Jerusalem to special quarters in the Temple. Towards the end of the Second Temple period, some of the High Priests were not very knowledgeable and had to be specially briefed to make sure that they did not make any mistakes. During this time he would perform the regular sacrifices and study the instructions concerning the rituals he was about to undertake. The High Priest was expected to stay awake all night on the eve of Yom Kippur, reading the scriptures. It was said that, if he started to doze, young priests would recite psalms very loudly, or stand him barefoot on a cold stone floor!

At dawn, he ritually bathed and put on a set of gold ritual garments. He performed the regular morning tasks of the priest: he made a sacrifice; tended the Menorah and burnt incense. He then took off the gold garments, bathed again and put on plain white linen garments. He went over to a young bull, placed his hands on his head and leaned on him. Here he recited the first of the three great confessions, this time for himself and his family. In his confession he addressed God as YHWH.[2] Yom Kippur was the only day when the divine name of God was permitted to be used and only by the High Priest. This was a spiritual high point for all present and many would prostrate themselves out of reverence to the name. Next he would be led over to two goats. By the means of lots, one was chosen to be a sacrifice and the other to be the scapegoat. He tied a red cord on the horns of the scapegoat and then returned to the bull. Leaning on him, he made a second confession, this time for the priests. He slaughtered the bull and collected the blood in a basin, which was stirred by another priest to stop it coagulating.

The High Priest's gown was fringed with pomegranates and bells, and the people could hear him moving around (Exodus 28:35). Some say that a rope was tied around his waist so that he could be pulled back if he was unable to stand the presence of God and was struck down when he entered the Holy of Holies. This moment had arrived. He took a golden pan in his right hand and used it to shovel up some of the burning embers at the altar. In his left hand, he took a golden ladle and filled it with incense. Then he walked towards the Holy of Holies. He entered and placed the embers in front of the Ark of the Covenant, between the two poles. He placed the incense on top of the coals and the chamber filled with smoke, which was supposed to prevent him looking upon the divine presence. As he left, he prayed for the welfare of the people, who were relieved to see his reappearance. He took some of the bull's blood and returned to the Holy of Holies where he sprinkled it towards (not on) the Ark – this was the sacrifice for himself and the priests. Next he slaughtered the goat, took its blood and sprinkled it in the same manner – this sacrifice was for the people. The remaining blood of the animals was mixed together and smeared on the altar. The High Priest's next task was to go to the scapegoat, and lean on it while he confessed the sins of the nation. A priest led it away into the desert to the cliff at Mount Azazel thought to be about twelve miles away. Here the red cord was divided into two. Half was left on the horns of the goat and half was tied to the cliff. The goat was pushed over the cliff backwards and perished.[3] Meanwhile the bull and sacrificial goat were drawn and their bodies taken outside the city and burned. The High Priest read and recited the sections of the Torah from Leviticus and Numbers that concerned Yom Kippur. He took off his linen garments and immersed himself for a third time before putting on golden garments. Now he offered two rams and burned the entrails of the bull and goat on the altar. He removed the gold robes, bathed again and put on white linen garments to enter the Holy of Holies for a final time to remove the incense and the golden pan with the burning coals. He returned to lead the daily afternoon service. First he needed to bathe for a fifth time and put on golden robes. He read the service, kindled the Menorah and burned incense on the incense altar.

Having completed all the rituals he washed his hands and his feet and was, finally, able to change into his own clothes and return to his own home. Here a feast was waiting for him.

So, with relief that the day had been accomplished without mishap, he could celebrate with his friends and family.

Yom Kippur in later Judaism

After the destruction of the Temple, the sacrifices could no longer be made for the sins of the nation. This might have been the end of the Day of Atonement, but Judaism had the scholarship and spirituality to overcome this great loss. While at Yavneh, the Sanhedrin reinterpreted Yom Kippur to retain significance in a non-sacrificial system.

The issue of repentance and atonement was a complex one but the rabbis believed that there were already precedents for non-sacrificial atonement in the Hebrew Bible. Did not the prophet Samuel say, 'To obey is better than sacrifice'? (1 Samuel 15:22). In Hosea they remembered the verse: 'Forgive all our sins and receive us graciously, that we may offer the fruit of our lips' (Hosea 14:2). In Hebrew the word translated as 'fruit' is literally 'young bulls'. They concluded that God required repentance ('teshuvah' in Hebrew) for forgiveness and this could be offered in place of the Temple sacrifices. Finally they found that the prophet Micah had considered whether God truly wanted burnt offerings and concluded that the Lord required his people 'to act justly and to love mercy and to walk humbly with your God' (Micah 6:8).

How could genuine repentance be achieved? The key verse is Leviticus 16:29. The King James Bible most faithfully conveys the Hebrew: 'In the seventh month on the tenth day of the month, ye shall afflict your souls and do no work at all.' The rabbis discussed how to 'afflict the soul' and decided that in addition to Sabbath regulations, five things were prohibited: eating and drinking; washing for pleasure; anointing; sexual relations; and wearing shoes and other items made from leather. These remain the basic requirements for Yom Kippur.

Although Christians and Jews have very different understanding of atonement, these sentiments have echoes in Jesus' teaching on the Law. In the Sermon on the Mount in particular, he places great emphasis on the importance of having the right inner attitude to God and to one's neighbour rather than simply keeping the letter of the Law.

Preparation for Yom Kippur

In Judaism, preparation for a festival is considered very important and this is especially true for the Day of Atonement. People prepare for Yom Kippur for forty days beforehand, first during the month of Elul, which they use as a period for self-examination. This is followed by Rosh Hashanah and the Days of Awe, when it is believed that the books of life and death are opened and a person's behaviour will determine where their name will be inscribed (see Chapter 4). Then comes the last day before the festival and a number of activities are required. Any outstanding debts must be paid and it is also traditional to give alms to a good cause. Orthodox Jews will ritually bathe in a mikvah or Jewish ritual bath. These are often located at the synagogue and mikvahs have been discovered when ancient synagogues are excavated. They have to have a fresh water source which is why many synagogues were located near a spring. Before sunset the final meal is eaten which is often a large one as it is a blessing to prepare well for the fast. Once the meal is over the table is cleared and in some homes a fresh cloth is laid and the Torah and prayer book are placed upon it. Thus the Torah becomes food. Memorial candles are lit in memory of the dead. The family put on fresh clothes, often white, and then, wearing canvas shoes without laces, they walk to the synagogue for the Kol Nidrei service.

Kol Nidrei ('All Vows')

This service starts before sundown and continues through the evening. It is a service for the cancellation of religious vows. The thinking is that, though each person may have tried to fulfil all their vows of the previous year, though they may have asked release from those they found they could not fulfil, there may still be some outstanding vows that they have overlooked. Kol Nidrei makes it possible to cancel these vows and have a clean sheet for the coming year. It is not a prayer but rather a legal formula. The Sephardi version gives remission from vows of the past, and the Ashkenazi version from those of the coming year. The origins of Kol Nidrei are lost in the mists of time. There is an unsubstantiated theory that it began in Spain for Jews who had been forced to convert to Christianity. By praying the Kol Nidrei prayer each year they could live outwardly as Christians and yet remain secretly Jewish. Just before Kol Nidrei, there is a prayer that allows those excommunicated from the community to rejoin. Sadly Kol Nidrei became the focus of anti-Semitism in the Middle Ages, when it was suggested that Jewish people might not keep their word. This led to great controversy over Kol Nidrei. It has been removed from some of the Reform prayer books and is sometimes prefaced by an explanation of the religious nature of the vows expiated. Despite this dilemma, the haunting melody of Kol Nidrei remains one of the most beautiful and best loved of all the synagogue prayers. In Kol Nidrei there is recognition that even our well–intended plans can go wrong. It is also a homecoming for those estranged from the community, and every year Jewish people will return to synagogue for Yom Kippur even though they may not have been seen there throughout the intervening twelve months.[4]

The day of fasting

Synagogue services continue throughout the day of Yom Kippur. There are five periods of prayer, which often run into each other. The passages concerning the Day of Atonement are read from the Pentateuch, together with Isaiah 57:14–58:14, the book of Jonah and Micah 7:18–20. All of these passages deal with fasting, repentance and forgiveness.

The end of the day

I once spent Yom Kippur in Jerusalem. The Jewish half of the city was almost totally quiet throughout the day. As with Shabbat, all public transport was stopped but on that day there were also almost no cars. (I have been told that among secular Jews it is known as 'Yom Video' as this is the only alternative if you do not want to keep the fast!) By late afternoon we decided to walk down to see the end of the day at the Western Wall in the Old City. Everybody seemed to be out on foot. There were women in long cotton dresses and men in white and other festival clothing, including large fur-rimmed hats, which are so reminiscent of Eastern Europe. The Western Wall (or Wailing Wall as it is sometimes called) is literally the western wall of the Temple Mount. As you approach it through the Jewish Quarter of the Old City, the Dome of the Rock begins to tower above. In front is a large plaza and we could see this filling with people as we waited to pass through the security gate on the steps. By the wall itself, there was a sense of expectancy. Soon this solemn day would be over and it would be time to rejoice. One elderly man in white, with a long grey beard and a prayer shawl, seemed impatient to see the end of the festival. When it was time he nudged a younger man in his group to blow the shofar to announce the end of the fast. Almost immediately the older man started to sing 'Am Yisrael chai' (the people of Israel live) and soon everyone seemed to be singing and dancing. The atmosphere was tremendous and I could share in the rejoicing that seemed ultimately to be at the heart of this solemn day. Eventually people drifted away for a light meal. On the following morning I saw small boys in the Jewish Quarter dragging long palm branches – they were already making preparations for their sukkah!

Yom Kippur in the New Testament

Jesus and Yom Kippur

Though there is no direct mention of Yom Kippur in the Gospels, I have become intrigued by Matthew 6 which echoes the themes of this period, and wonder whether Jesus may have been making reference to the autumn festivals here. Jesus instructs people not to give alms in public, especially by announcing their gift with trumpets. For Matthew's Jewish Christian readers, the mention of almsgiving together with the shofar may well have taken their thoughts to the High Holy Days and the eve of Yom Kippur. Jesus was making a distinction between those looking for reward in this life (to be in the book of life in the coming year?) and those who were looking for eternal life. If we consider the rest of this chapter we find that it continues the Yom Kippur themes. First, there is a section on prayer, including the Lord's Prayer, which has similarities to Jewish prayer patterns and involves prayer for repentance and forgiveness.[5] Secondly, there is a section on fasting, suggesting both washing and anointing to make the fast secret. These instructions might have been a reaction against excessive public displays by the more extreme of the Pharisees. The overall teaching by Jesus is that prayer, repentance, fasting and giving to the needy should be private not public, and that our focus should be on the world to come rather than material reward in this life.

We cannot know whether this was a Yom Kippur sermon by Jesus, or used as such by his Jewish followers. From modern scholarship we can deduce that it would have fitted within the range of contemporary debate about the Judaism of Jesus' day.[6] We have seen that the rabbis at Yavneh also felt that inner repentance was at the heart of the Day of Atonement. If Matthew 6 were used as a Yom Kippur discourse, it would undoubtedly have been a great challenge to those who thought that simply observing the festival was enough.[7]

Yom Kippur is the certain background for the teaching of Hebrews 9. Here the Tabernacle on earth is described as a copy of a far greater one in heaven (verse 11). Every year the High Priest needed to atone for the sins of the people with a sacrifice, but Jesus suffered once to take away the sins of all (verse 28). In this passage Jesus is both the High Priest and the sacrifice.[8]

Jewish and Christian views of atonement

The issues of repentance and forgiveness of sin are the central themes of Yom Kippur, and from it we can learn much about the different Jewish and Christian views of atonement. Jewish theology teaches that observing Yom Kippur atones for sin and that this is received through prayer and repentance.[9] Christians believe that there cannot be forgiveness of sin without a sacrifice, and see the death and resurrection of Jesus as the ultimate sacrifice, which atoned for sin. Repentance and the receiving of forgiveness by grace are the means by which we enter into this atonement. When we understand the difference in these views, Christians might appreciate why some Jewish people would believe that, at Yavneh, Judaism moved on from a rather 'primitive' idea of blood sacrifice to a 'higher' religious ideal of repentance. Likewise, Jewish people may understand why Christians see the death of Jesus to be absolutely central to their faith and to be the only means by which we can gain peace with God.

Making the link

In these differing views of repentance and forgiveness we find both the link and the divide between Christianity and Judaism. Both are based on the same Old Testament scriptures, both see God as creator and redeemer, but in the first century each took a different view of this core subject. The

Christian view was arguably no less Jewish from a first-century perspective. The Hebrew scriptures were central to New Testament belief, and we see examples in the Ethiopian eunuch reading Isaiah 53 recorded in Acts 8, and with Jesus who quoted Psalm 22 from the cross. As the church progressed, however, these concepts were transmitted in Greek and began to lose their Hebraic feel. For the Jews who did not follow Jesus, the strand of Jewish teaching that he represented was, not surprisingly, left behind. As the emerging church became increasingly anti-Jewish in its outlook and actions, Jewish theology responded by defining a view that was distinct from the Christian one. One of the services on Yom Kippur focuses on ten rabbis who were martyred by the Romans. It is thought to have been added during the Crusades to give courage following the massacres of Jewish people by the Crusader armies.

Christians often ask me why Jewish people do not believe that Jesus is their Messiah. An understanding of the history of the church and its actions towards Jewish people over the centuries begins to give the answer to this question, and various chapters of this book explain different aspects. I have heard Jewish followers of Jesus use the story of Joseph in the book of Genesis to explain how Jewish people view Jesus. When Joseph's brothers came to see him, they did not recognise him because of his Egyptian dress and language and manners. In the same way, the church has made Jesus appear very Gentile and it is sometimes hard to see the Jewish person underneath. On this the greatest day in the Jewish calendar, it is appropriate for Christians to reflect on their history regarding Jewish people. We can pray that, despite the atrocities of our forebears and our own shortcomings, we might bring an understanding of the love and forgiveness of our Jewish Messiah to his own people.

A day to pray and reflect

Many Christians are finding benefit from taking a day out to pray and reflect. This might be in an organised day on your own or with a group. There are now a large number of Christian centres offering days of this type for which they provide a programme based around a particular theme. Groups can organise their own speaker and programme. One example is a Tuesday morning parents (mostly mums) group in our church, which organises an annual quiet day in a local Christian centre. They book a speaker, arrange to leave the children behind, and give themselves the luxury of a whole day to pray and reflect together.

If you have already experienced group and organised days you may value a day of prayer on your own. It is important to go away somewhere, since you will have too many distractions in your own home. Many of the centres who offer group retreats will also provide a room for this. You will find it helpful to have a framework for your day. You might decide to read through a book of the Bible or a devotional book which you have been wanting to read but have not had time for. If you take a biblical book it is sometimes helpful to find a short commentary or a linked Bible study book. I also take a pen and a notebook and sometimes a prayer book or a song book. How much do you want to be absolutely on your own? Some centres have group worship times, and many individuals will find these helpful. These are rarely obligatory, however, and others may prefer to stay apart. Most will provide meals, but will also be happy for individuals to bring food to eat alone or to fast.

I generally structure my day by starting with worship, giving time for my mind to slow down and concentrate. I will then turn to the book or section of a book of the Bible that I have chosen for that day. Usually I will read straight through first of all, noting down any particular verses or themes that emerge. This gives an overview of a book which can be lost in more detailed study. From this point, I start to let the themes from scripture 'interact' with the thoughts, concerns and questions that I have brought to the day. After a break for more prayer or worship (or sometimes coffee!), I go back to the beginning and go over the same material much more slowly, using a commentary or Bible study book if I have one. It is useful to continue to make notes, to pray and reflect as you go along and also give space just 'to be'. This whole period can also be interspersed with breaks and usually goes on at least until midday. I generally take a walk in the afternoon, when I frequently find that my thoughts are inspired through the natural world. Then I return and spend the final hour or so seeking to draw the day together. How has God been speaking to me? How have I responded? What are the things that I need to take away from the day and put into practice?

Make a felt book jacket for your Bible

This solves the problem of a Bible whose hard cover has begun to fall off and can only be repaired through unsightly tape. An attractive outer jacket will restore its appearance and personalise your Bible. At Yom Kippur the Torah is placed on the table as a symbol that God's word has replaced physical food. This makes it an appropriate time to give your treasured old Bible a 'face-lift'. I have given the instructions for felt, but you could also use soft leather if you have any available. In this case it is advisable to use a special leather needle which you can purchase through specialist craft shops, and use button thread for extra strength.

You will need:
One large piece of felt big enough to easily fit round your Bible with about 5 in (12 cm) extra in width
Scraps of felt in at least one other colour
Needle and thread of matching colours
A pair of scissors and pins
Tailor's chalk or a ballpoint pen.

Fold the piece of felt around your Bible and mark with pins a line ⅜ in (½ cm) above and below the height of the book and 2½ in (6 cm) longer than the width at either end. Remove the felt and place on a flat surface. Using a ruler, mark out the rectanglar shape that will make the outline of your jacket. Before you cut it out, check again by wrapping it around your Bible. The outside of the book should be completely covered apart from where the pages open. There should be ⅜ in (½ cm) extra at the top and the bottom and 2½ in (6 cm) at either end where the cover opens for the pages (this will be folded around the cover and will be sewn top and bottom to make the jacket stay on). Cut out your felt and pin 2½ in (6 cm) inwards at either end. Sew these with matching thread.

Next draw out your design on paper. I have chosen an ancient Jewish symbol of the two stone tablets containing the Ten Commandments. Cut out the paper and then pin onto a different colour felt. Cut out this design and pin onto the front of your cover. Make sure it is in the right place by fitting the jacket onto your Bible. Adjust if necessary and then remove and sew. Refit and your new jacket is complete.

Youth track

Prayers for world peace

This is a great time of year to pray for world peace. One day Jesus will return and he will bring complete peace on earth. Until that time, we need to pray for peace and for God's sovereignty among the nations. You might like to research one country of the world where there is a problem with peace. You could look for cuttings from newspapers or news magazines and make up a poster giving information about it. What specific things does this country need prayer for? How could you raise awareness of the problems of this country in your church or school?

Recipe

Sephardi Salmon

This recipe is great served with a crunchy green salad and warm fresh bread. It would be suitable for any of the autumn festivals but is particularly good for breaking the Yom Kippur fast because it is both light to eat and quick to prepare.

For 2 people
2 salmon fillets
1 large clove of garlic, crushed
1 dessertspoon wholemeal flour
1 tablespoon olive oil

½ oz (20 g) pine nuts
½ oz (20 g) sultanas
1 dessertspoon lemon juice
1 tablespoon white wine or sherry
1 large teaspoon honey
2 fl oz (50 ml) water
Fresh chopped herbs to garnish (e.g. lemon balm, parsley, coriander or dill)

Wash and dry the salmon pieces and then toss in the wholemeal flour. Heat the oil in a large frying pan or wok and then lightly fry the salmon with the crushed garlic for 10 minutes until almost cooked (turn the fillets over while cooking). Meanwhile, gently toast the pine nuts (I usually put them on a shallow metal container and place under the grill for a few minutes). Add the lemon juice, wine, honey and water to the pan and gently mix with the salmon, turning them on both sides to mix in the flour coating. Add the nuts and sultanas and mix into the sauce. Simmer uncovered for a further 5–10 minutes or so until the liquid has reduced and thickened and the fish has absorbed the flavours. If you are not ready to eat it immediately, transfer to a covered baking dish and keep warm in a cool to moderate oven. Serve with the sauce spooned over the fillets and garnished with chopped fresh herbs, if available.

Notes

1. Exodus 30:10; Leviticus 16.
2. Jewish people never pronounce the divine name of God. Therefore, as Hebrew has no vowels, I have simply transliterated the consonants.
3. There is a rabbinic legend that the cord would turn white as a sign that the sins of the people had been atoned for. Edersheim maintained that in the final forty years of the

Temple (after the death of Jesus) the cord did not turn white. Edersheim, A., *The Temple* (The Religious Tract Society: London, c.1880) p. 312.
4. Strassfeld, M., *The Jewish Holidays, A Guide and Commentary* (Harper and Row: New York, 1985), pp.113ff.
5. Wilson, M., *Our Father Abraham* (Wm. B. Eerdmans Publishing Company: Grand Rapids, MI, 1989), pp. 117–118. See also Young, B., *The Jewish Background to the Lord's Prayer* (Center for Judaic-Christian Studies: Austin, TX, 1984) for a good explanation of the Jewish background to this prayer.
6. Sanders, E. P., *Jewish Law from Jesus to the Mishnah*. (SCM Press: London, and Trinity Press International: Philadelphia, 1990), p. 23.
7. Young, B., *The Parables, Jewish Tradition and Christian Interpretation* (Hendrickson Publishers: Massachusetts, 1998), p.129, is the only reference I have found to mention a probable Yom Kippur connection.
8. An extended discussion of the Day of Atonement and Hebrews 9 is given in Hughes, P. E., *A Commentary on the Epistle to the Hebrews* (Wm. B. Eerdmans Publishing Company: Grand Rapids, MI, 1977), pp. 306ff.
9. There are passages in the Talmud that say the shedding of blood is required for forgiveness, but this did not become the accepted Jewish position on the means of atonement.

Chapter Six

TABERNACLES – JESUS COMING AMONG US

My first ever visit to Israel on my own was in the autumn. I had visited the country before, but only as part of a group. This visit was my first experience of Israel off the tourist track. As I arrived in Jerusalem on the local 'Egged' bus, it seemed to have undergone a transformation. On every balcony, temporary shelters had been made out of boards, branches and anything else that came to hand. It was as if the city had suddenly turned into a mass refugee camp and a stranger might have imagined that just such an event had occurred, the extra people being housed in the shelters. This was, of course, the Feast of Tabernacles, or Sukkot as it is known in Hebrew. The shelters (tabernacles) were not for unexpected refugees but for local families to live in for a week. In this way they would remind themselves that they too had once been refugees and God's hand had brought them to this land.

Three elements of the festival

The Feast of Tabernacles is the third pilgrimage festival. It is the final harvest festival, when all the crops are gathered in.

For the ancient Israelites, Sukkot was so important that it was simply known as the Feast (Deuteronomy 16:15). The basic instructions for Tabernacles are found in Leviticus 23. It is celebrated for seven days, starting on the fifteenth day of the seventh month, which is the month of Tishri (September or October). The first day should be a Sabbath and the eighth day, after the end of the festival, should also be a Sabbath. Leviticus then goes on to outline special fruits that should be used in the festival, and instructions on how to build a temporary shelter called a tabernacle or sukkah.

Building a tabernacle

The centre of celebration for this festival is the tabernacle. This has to be a temporary structure and there are many rules about its construction. It is only allowed to have one permanent wall, which does mean that it can be built up against a house. Today the walls might be made of hardboard or plastic sheeting over a frame. The roof is made of branches sparse enough to be able to see the stars. You are not allowed to cover the roof with any waterproof material. Once these basic rules have been observed, the sukkah can then be decorated. It is traditional to hang fruit from the roof, and the walls are usually decorated with bright pictures. The sukkah is used for eating meals and for study. Some families will sleep in it for at least one night. This obviously lends itself well to a hot country such as Israel, other parts of the Mediterranean or even California. It is not so suitable for colder countries such as Britain and particularly Eastern Europe.

The four species

Four special fruits are mentioned: 'Fruits from the goodly trees, branches of palm trees, boughs of leafy trees and willow of the brook' (Leviticus 23:40, RSV). These were to be used to rejoice before the Lord. The Talmud identified the boughs of leafy trees as myrtle, and the 'fruits from the goodly trees' as a citrus called an etrog. This looks like a large lemon, with a prominent tip or 'pittom'. The palm branch, which should be beautiful, has a holder made out of the base of it. Here are placed the willow and myrtle. These are held with the etrog and shaken to the four points of the globe, upwards and downwards, while a blessing is recited.

It is not known why these particular four species were commanded to be waved. Over the generations many traditions have grown up concerning them. One tradition sees the four fruits as symbolic of the four stages of coming into the land. The palm trees are symbolic of the desert; the willows of the Jordan River and the way into the Promised Land; the myrtle of the forested hillsides, and finally the etrog symbolises the fertile plains of Israel.

Another tradition links the four species to four different types of people. Dates from the palm tree have taste but no smell: this is symbolic of people who are very clever but rather impractical. The myrtle has a lovely fragrance but no taste: this represents people who are practical, and always willing to help others, but are not very clever. The willow has neither taste nor fragrance: this is symbolic of people who are 'good for nothing'! Finally, the etrog has a wonderful fragrance and a good taste: this is symbolic of people who are not only very learned but are also full of good deeds. The punch line of the story is to thank God that he has not made everybody to be an etrog! Most people have their weaknesses, and all types of people are needed to make up a genuine community.

Rejoicing

The third activity of the festival is to rejoice. This is commanded in Leviticus 23. Verse 40 says: 'On the first day, you are to take choice fruits from the trees, and palm fronds, leafy branches, and poplars, and rejoice before the Lord your God for seven days.' Throughout the biblical period we find that this is the most joyful of all festivals. Sometimes Tabernacles became too joyful and the prophets warn about over-indulgence.

Harvest or wilderness?

Tabernacles contains both a harvest and a wilderness theme. The major traditions about Sukkot concern the Israelites wandering in the wilderness. As the Israelites made shelters and lived in these for a week they reminded themselves that they were once without homes and in the desert. Sukkot is also the Feast of Ingathering (Exodus 23). Harvest festivals were known in many cultures in the Ancient Near East, and Judges 9:27 describes a Canaanite harvest festival at this time of year. The Israelites would have almost certainly lived in tents in the desert, but the tabernacles, described above, are more akin to shelters in a harvest field than to tents. This could place the roots of the festival in the cyclical agricultural year rather than the historical pilgrimage of the Jewish people. Could they have borrowed this festival from the Canaanites after they arrived in Canaan? Some of the later revelry condemned by the prophets may have come from the Canaanite traditions, but there is no record of booths as part of the Canaanites' festival. It seems odd, moreover, to expect a farmer to return to his field hut for a week after finishing the harvest – why? Leviticus 23:42–43 states that: 'All native born Israelites are to live in booths so that your descendants will know that I made the Israelites live in booths when I brought them out of Egypt.'

Nogah Hareuveni suggests a possible solution.[1] The traditional nomadic people in the desert, the Bedouin, use tents for most of the year and not shelters. In the autumn, however, the pasture land and desert cisterns have been used up. At this time of year these shepherds gather together at a date palm oasis where they can also harvest the dates. Shelters are made from the palm branches and so Bedouin traditionally live in booths, not tents, in this autumn season.

It may be that, in God's command to live in booths, the Israelites were not only remembering that they were once nomads in the wilderness, but were especially remembering the autumn time of joy when they would rest for a while at an oasis of date palms. The abundant water and harvest of sweet fruits reminded them of God's generous provision for them.

Tabernacles in Temple times

Sukkot had a very special connection with the Temple because Solomon dedicated the Temple during Sukkot. In 1 Kings 8 there is a full description of this event. First, the Ark containing the stone tablets of the covenant was brought into the newly completed Holy of Holies. The chapter continues: 'When the priests withdrew from the Holy Place, the cloud filled the Temple of the Lord. And the priests could not perform their service because of the cloud, for the glory of the Lord filled his Temple' (1 Kings 8:10–11). King Solomon then prayed to the Lord and the Temple was dedicated with sacrifices and much rejoicing. They celebrated the festival of Sukkot with so much rejoicing that, after the first seven days, they continued the festival for a further seven days (1 Kings 8:65). The cloud filling the Temple was the Shekinah, or the Glory of the Lord. As we discovered in Chapter 3, this was a visible sign of God's presence and was also reminiscent of the cloud coming on Mount Sinai and descending on the Tabernacle in the wilderness.

By Solomon's day there was a strong tradition of the three annual feasts: Passover, Pentecost and Tabernacles (2 Chronicles 8:13). In later centuries, as the nation fell into decline, it appears that these festivals also fell into disuse with only the revival of Passover by kings Hezekiah and Josiah. We do not encounter Sukkot again until Nehemiah's restoration of Jerusalem several generations later. It appears that the festival was not observed, or possibly took on some of the excesses of the Canaanite harvest feast and so became more of a pagan festival. There are many warnings from prophets such as Hosea and Amos that God would judge Israel for the excesses at her appointed feasts and her lack of focus on him (for example Hosea 2:10–12). God warns that he will bring Israel back to her true festivals: 'I will make you live in tents again, as in the days of your appointed feasts' (Hosea 12:9). In this way God reminds his people that he was the one who brought them out of Egypt and sustains them in the Promised Land.

The continued disobedience of the people led to the exile in Babylon. Without the land and the Temple, the Jews turned to study and to prayer. A very different spirit pervaded those returning to Israel and they sought to revive the ancient Feasts of the Lord. In Nehemiah 8 there is a description of Ezra, the scribe, gathering the people and reading the Bible (Torah) to them. Discovering that they should be celebrating the Feast of Tabernacles, they were commanded to rejoice and to make booths for themselves. Verse 17 records that the festival had not been celebrated so fully since the days of Joshua – it was a period of very great joy for them.

Sukkot continued to be celebrated throughout the time of the Second Temple, only ceasing during the time when the Greeks defiled the Temple. The Maccabees rose up against the Greeks, to regain Jerusalem in 164 BC. They broke with tradition and continued to fight during the Feast of Tabernacles. When they regained the city and cleansed the Temple, their rededication was a late Sukkot celebration (2 Maccabees 10:1–8). This new festival of Hanukkah (Chapter 7) contained many of the Tabernacles traditions.

Tabernacles in the New Testament

The rededicated Second Temple provided the focus for the three great festivals once again. By New Testament times they were well established as the great religious events of the year.

Passover and Tabernacles were the two great festivals and Pentecost did not play such a significant role at that time. Passover was probably the most popular but Tabernacles was also very significant and would attract Jewish people from all over the Diaspora. Traditions had grown with the centuries though the three elements – booths, the four species, and a feast of joy – remained.

Most of the ceremonies focused on the Temple. Willow branches decorated the altar, with their points facing inwards. The priests would bring palms and willows to the Temple and wave them each day while circling the altar once, reciting psalms and blowing silver trumpets. On the last (seventh) day of the festival, five willows were bound together and carried round the altar seven times. As they circled the altar they sang from the Hallel Psalms (113–118, 136), but especially emphasised Psalm 118:25: 'O Lord save us (Hosannah); O Lord give us success.' Because of this, the final day became known as the 'Great Day' or the 'Great Hosannah'. The willow branches would be shaken and beaten until all the leaves had been lost from them and palm branches were also waved. The beating and waving of the four species sounds a little like rain falling and this ceremony was a prayer for the autumn rains to come.

Water is a key element for the Festival of Sukkot. Jerusalem has always struggled to have enough water. There is only one spring, called Gihon, which is outside the city in the Kidron valley. There was an ancient tunnel built from within the city walls to this spring which was used by King David to enter and conquer the city. King Hezekiah built a second tunnel to take the water from the spring to a pool, called Siloam, which was within the city to the south of the Temple.

The Festival of Tabernacles comes in the autumn and by this time of year there has not been rain for many months. Praying for rain became a central part of the Sukkot festivities. On each day of the Festival, the priests would go down to the Pool of Siloam with a golden horn which they would fill with water. They would then return to the Temple with much rejoicing, singing the Hallel Psalms. They poured out water onto the altar and prayed for the autumn rains to come. This was known as the Libation Ceremony and was based on Isaiah 12:3: 'With joy you shall draw water from the wells of salvation.'

The second major theme for Sukkot in New Testament times was light. This probably came from the description of the Shekinah or Glory of the Lord appearing at Tabernacles time when the Temple was first dedicated. During the Second Temple period, a special ceremony was enacted in the Court of the Women. In each corner of the court, four huge candlesticks were erected. Each had four branches with large bowls filled with olive oil. Each bowl contained a wick, which was made out of the worn–out garments of the priests. These were lit at night, so illuminating the Temple with sixteen torches. In the days before floodlighting the effect was quite breathtaking for the pilgrims and residents of the city. Each household also had torches in their own courtyards. Under these lights the people gathered for an evening of praise. It was said by the rabbis that whoever had not celebrated Tabernacles in Jerusalem had never experienced real joy.

Jesus at the Feast of Tabernacles

There is one definite incident of Jesus attending the Feast of Tabernacles and this is found in John 7–8. Jesus' brothers challenged him to come with them to the Feast, but he was reluctant to go. This might seem surprising, but the reason becomes clear if we remember the link between Sukkot and the Maccabean revolt. The people of Jesus' day were looking for a Messiah who would be like the Maccabees and would fight to regain Israel from their oppressors. Jesus knew that, if he came publicly to Jerusalem at this time, he would be proclaimed 'King Messiah' and would become the focus of a revolt. He stayed in Galilee a few days longer and so did not arrive in Jerusalem until the middle of feast. Rather than make a big messianic arrival, he instead took up his role as a rabbi and began to teach in the Temple courts. His teaching caused great controversy, partly because of his great learning but mainly because of his claims about himself. Then, on the final day of the festival, Jesus made a dramatic statement. This was the day when, after the Libation Ceremony, the priests would circle the altar seven times and would make the special entreaty to the Lord to save them and to give them the autumn rains. We read in John 7:37–38:

> On the last and greatest day of the feast, Jesus stood up and said in a loud voice, 'If any one is thirsty, let him come to me and drink. Whoever believes in me, as the scripture has said, streams of living water will flow from within him.'

It is a hard at this distance to imagine how dramatic and how shocking this statement was. It is no wonder that, as a result, some people called him a prophet, some the Messiah, but that others wanted to seize him as a heretic.

Jesus' second statement at this festival was no less dramatic, especially when we realise that he was actually in the floodlit Temple when he made the statement. John 8:12 describes the scene: 'When Jesus spoke again to the people, he said, "I am the light of the world. Whoever follows me will never walk in darkness, but will have the light of life."' Given the festival lights and their link to the Shekinah, it is no wonder that Jesus was accused of claiming equality with God. This was exactly what he was doing.

So in these two statements we see Jesus not taking the role of a gentle teacher but of a very bold and controversial prophet. His listeners were left with two alternatives, either he was the Messiah and the Son of God, or he was an impostor and a dangerous blasphemer.

Jesus tabernacled among us

John's Gospel gives another key passage that connects Jesus with Tabernacles. John 1:14 says: 'The Word became flesh and tabernacled among us. We have seen his glory, the glory of the one and only who came from the Father, full of grace and truth.' The word which here is 'tabernacled' is sometimes translated as 'dwelt among us' or 'made his home among us'. The Greek literally says 'pitched his tent among us'. To John's Jewish listeners this would have led them to think of the holy Tabernacle in the wilderness. Just as God was very centrally and very specially present during the wilderness wanderings of the Jewish people, so Jesus especially came among us to live on earth. 'God with us' is a High Holy Days theme and links Sukkot with the incarnation of Jesus. Many Christians believe that Jesus was born at Sukkot time rather than in December. This is because of calculations regarding when the 'bright star' might have appeared. Certainly the themes of God dwelling among us, of spiritual refreshment, and of great joy, are common to both Sukkot in the Jewish calendar and Christmas in the Christian calendar. Sukkot is preceded by a period of self-examination, mindful of the judgement of God. Likewise, Advent is a period of preparation when we are aware of God's judgement as well as his overwhelming mercy in sending us Jesus.

Tabernacles to come

We have seen that Passover was fulfilled in the death and resurrection of Jesus, Pentecost was fulfilled in the coming of the Holy Spirit, but there is a fulfilment of Tabernacles which is still to come. Jesus has tabernacled among us once in his birth and life on earth, but he has promised to return.

Many people also link the return of Jesus with the Feast of Tabernacles. Why is this? If we look at the Old Testament we find that there are two strands to the messianic hope. One involves the Suffering Servant and is typified by Isaiah 53. Here the Messiah suffers and dies for his people to bring them redemption. 'He was pierced for our transgressions, he was crushed for our iniquities; the punishment that brought us peace was upon him, and by his wounds we are healed' (Isaiah 53:5).

The second strand describes a King Messiah and is typified by Isaiah 11. In this passage, the Messiah regathers his people, there is a final judgement and he brings about peace on earth.

> The wolf will lie with the lamb, the leopard will lie down with the goat ... In that day the root of Jesse will stand as a banner for the peoples, the nations will rally to him, and his place of rest will be glorious. In that day the Lord will reach out his hand a second time to reclaim the remnant that is left of his people. (Isaiah 11:6, 10–11)

In the early centuries of the Christian era there was a Jewish tradition of two Messiahs. Messiah Ben Joseph would be a suffering servant who would die for his people and Messiah Ben David would be a King Messiah who would restore his people and bring about peace on earth. This is recorded in the Jerusalem Talmud.[2] Later Judaism applied the suffering servant theme to Israel and the messianic hope to a Messiah who would be king.

Christians see these two strands as two stages of Jesus' mission. His first coming among us was as a Suffering Servant. He pitched his tent among us and identified with us. He suffered on our behalf to bring about our redemption. His second coming will be in glory as King Messiah to bring about the final ingathering, judge the earth and establish eternal peace.

How does it relate to Tabernacles? Jesus' first coming as the Suffering Servant fulfilled the Passover festival with its themes of sacrifice and redemption. His second coming as King Messiah can be shown to fulfil the Feast of Tabernacles. Many of the passages concerning the Second Coming of Jesus in the New Testament and of the King Messiah in the Old Testament contain Tabernacles and High Holy Days themes. 1 Thessalonians 4:16 describes the return of Christ to be announced by the sounding of a trumpet and, as we saw in Chapter 4, this links to Rosh Hashanah. At the start of the High Holy Days, we hear the trumpet blast to prepare for God's judgement at Yom Kippur, and God's presence among us at Sukkot. When Jesus returns we will also hear the trumpet as we prepare for judgement and to meet our God.

Revelation 7 describes the final redemption of Christ very vividly. This scene is reminiscent of rejoicing in the Temple at Tabernacles:

> After this I looked and there before me was a great multitude that no one could count, from every nation, tribe, people and language, standing before the throne and in front of the Lamb. They were wearing white robes and were holding palm branches in their hands. And they cried out in a loud voice: 'Salvation (Hosannah) belongs to our God, who sits on the throne and to the Lamb.' (Revelation 7:9–10)

Jerusalem will have eternal light and water will flow from the throne out through the city.[3] The passage from Isaiah 11, quoted above, has many themes in common with Tabernacles and the return of Jesus, particularly ingathering, rejoicing and judgement. The Old Testament also gives a picture of the Festival of Tabernacles in the last days. The Feast will continue with all nations taking part. Zechariah 14 sees into the future: 'Then the survivors from all the nations that have attacked Jerusalem will go up year after year to worship the King, the Lord Almighty, and to celebrate the Feast of Tabernacles' (Zechariah 14:16).

From these passages we can conclude that in the return of Jesus there will be an ultimate fulfilment of the Feast of Tabernacles. First there will be judgement. This will be followed by a time of unimaginable joy, and of a final ingathering of God's people. The redeemed will live with the eternal presence of God's Shekinah light and be refreshed by the living water of the Holy Spirit.

Sukkot in later Judaism

Sukkot could not be such a magnificent festival after the destruction of the Temple, but it still remained the most joyful of all the Jewish festivals. Because Sukkot had an emphasis on being exiles in the wilderness, living in temporary dwellings, it lent itself well to the Diaspora and many of the traditions continued. Jewish people in all countries continued to build booths. Often the climate did not lend itself to this aspect of the festival and, as previously stated, this would have been particularly true in Eastern Europe where there were large Jewish populations up until the Second World War. The rabbis decreed that Sukkot should be a festival of joy, not of endurance. For this reason, there were minimum obligations for the use of the sukkah, and it was commanded that you should not exceed these if it would diminish your enjoyment of the festival. The sukkah was traditionally used for eating, sleeping, and study. If it was raining, it was only necessary to eat a token meal even on the first night, when blessings would be said over the wine and the bread in the sukkah, but the rest of the meal could be eaten in the dry. This is the opposite to the usual attitude to the law that 'puts a fence around the Torah' and encourages people to go beyond the minimum ruling. On Sukkot, all should rejoice whatever the weather.

In climates which did lend themselves to Sukkot, the sukkah was (and is) used for every meal. It genuinely became a temporary home, with pictures, carpets and furniture. In Israel today, cafes and restaurants erect Sukkot over their outdoor tables. Children will sleep in the family sukkah, and parents will study in them.

The four species continued to be used after the destruction of the Temple. Willow and myrtle were easy to come by in most countries. Palm branches were a little more difficult in cooler climates, and etrogs had to be imported from the Holy Land. In many communities only the well-off had their own four species, and there were community ones available for those who could not afford their own. The branches were waved in the synagogue rather than the Temple. With the re-establishment of the State of Israel, the Western Wall of the Temple Mount has gained importance as a place of prayer. On Sukkot, the four species are used in prayer here and special booths are available for public use.

By the Middle Ages, the seventh day of Tabernacles, the Great Hosannah or Hosannah Rabbah, had become more like the Days of Awe or a second Yom Kippur, especially among Sephardim. Just as with the Temple, it became traditional to walk around the inside of the synagogue once on every other day in Sukkot but seven times on Hosannah Rabbah. After this willow branches were taken and beaten on the ground. There is a strong association with judgement and the service is a solemn one. Some part of the night is spent in prayer and study. A particular theme is Deuteronomy, and this has to be finished before starting the lectionary again at the beginning of the Torah. The book of Ecclesiastes is traditionally read on Sukkot. It is thought that this is because of its emphasis on the transitory nature of this world and the need to fix our eyes on the Lord.

There is a strong tradition of hospitality during Sukkot. As well as meals, people often drop in simply for a glass of wine and a cake. The kabbalists of Safed had imaginary 'guests' (Ushpizin). These were Abraham, Isaac, Jacob, Moses, Aaron, Joseph and David. They were said to represent the characteristics of loving kindness, power, beauty, victory, splendour, foundation, and sovereignty. They were also all wanderers and exiles and so fitted the Sukkot theme. A different guest was invited on each day and families had a special chair for their biblical guest. Some modern Reform and Liberal Jews also invite the prominent Jewish women of the Bible such as Sarah, Rebekkah, Rachel, Leah, Miriam, Abigail and Esther.

A recent development in Reform Judaism has been to consider the issue of homelessness.[4] The parallel to the Feast of Tabernacles is obvious and it is, therefore, a very appropriate time of year to remember the homeless in our cities. Maybe lunches are laid on for these modern 'ushpizin', or perhaps gifts are made to charities for the homeless both locally and overseas.

Simchat Torah, Shemini Atzeret

This is the eighth day from the start of Tabernacles. It has two Hebrew names. 'Shemini Atzeret' literally means the 'Eighth Assembly' and it refers to its origin as the day to tarry for a little longer in God's presence even though the festival has ended. 'Simchat Torah' means 'a rejoicing in the law' and this refers to the joyful ceremonies associated with beginning the cycle of readings at the start of the Torah again. There is the prayer for rain, which dates back to Temple times; but the main focus is upon giving thanks for the Torah. This is a post-biblical festival and probably dates from the tenth century. The Torah scrolls are removed from the Ark (the cupboard at the front of the synagogue) and are processed around the synagogue amid great praise. One person, known as the 'bridegroom of the Torah', is called up to the Bimah (central reading platform) to read the last part of Deuteronomy. A second person, known as the 'bridegroom of Genesis', is called to read the start of the book of Genesis. Thus, Simchat Torah marks the final transition from a harvest festival to one that gives thanks for God's word.

Making the link

What can this festival say to Christians? The symbol of the booth is a very powerful one. It can remind us, too, of the homelessness in our midst, and of the refugees in many parts of the world today. It can remind us of the Jewish historical experience of homelessness, which has sadly often come from being expelled from Christian towns and countries. It also reminds us of Jesus, both as he has come among us in his birth (soon becoming a refugee himself), and that he will come again in glory and with judgement to raise his people into eternal joy. This is a festival of light and of water, when we need to pray for the living water of the Holy Spirit to enable us to be a beacon for God's light in the world. It is a harvest festival, when we can thank God for all that he has provided for us.

The Feast of Tabernacles fell into disuse for much of the biblical period, later to be revived as a major festival. Perhaps the themes of Tabernacles could give a biblical depth that might help revive Christian harvest festival weekends, so often flagging in urban and suburban churches. We too can rejoice!

Preparing for Sukkot

The Feast of Tabernacles is one of my favourite Jewish festivals. Maybe it is the idea of camping in a tent that is more like an inside-out Christmas tree! If you are able to build a sukkah in your own garden or even at your church, you will be able to get some feeling of what this festival is all about. Building a structure up against a house with patio doors is the most practical. Some form of structure can be made with beanpoles, though more substantial wood or boarding is needed to make a shelter you can guarantee not to fall down. Another idea is to use the frame of a tent. Sukkah building can become a den building competition for children. However the booth is made, the roof needs to be open to the air. I usually use beanpoles for this and then cover them with branches. Fruit is hung from the roof and decorations are put up inside. Modern Reform synagogues sometimes build tabernacles indoors. This is also possible in church and can be a suitable focus for harvest offerings.[5]

Making a gingerbread tabernacle

You will need:

Three gingerbread walls (see recipe below). One should be roughly 6 in by 10 in (15 cm by 25 cm) and two should be roughly 6 in by 6 in (15 cm by 15 cm)
A cake board or an old bread board
About 2 oz of spaghetti, preferably just longer than 10 in (25 cm)
Some small sweets or marzipan
Small pictures from magazines
Icing and food colouring

A piping cone
Small 'branches' of herbs such as rosemary about 7 in (18 cm) long.

Position your gingerbread walls on the cake stand to make up three sides of a box, with the longest side at the back. Cement in place by piping icing along the bottom edges of the pieces and the sides that touch each other. Decorate the walls with the small pictures – these can also be held in place with icing.

The spaghetti makes up the roof, resting on the side walls. The roof decorations are added as the roof is made. Cut lengths of spaghetti that are just a little longer than the back wall. Gradually make the roof by cementing spaghetti across the side walls, building up from back to front. At the same time, make the hanging decorations from the roof by cementing sweets to the underside of the spaghetti (or by making fruit using marzipan or icing coloured with food colouring). This can be done after the roof is complete but it is a bit fiddly. Cut the rosemary twigs or other herbs to just overlap when placed from front to back of the sukkah. Rest these on top of the spaghetti to complete the tabernacle.

You may like to make the inside of the sukkah more elaborate: you could make a carpet out of marzipan; a doll's house table and chairs should fit inside; and the really adventurous could make people out of fondant icing.

Gingerbread walls

12 oz (340 g) plain flour
3 oz (85 g) soft brown sugar
3 oz (85 g) margarine
2 tablespoons golden syrup
1 tablespoon black treacle
3 teaspoons ginger
2 teaspoons cinnamon
1½ teaspoons baking powder

1 beaten egg
1–2 tablespoons milk

Sift the flour with the ginger, cinnamon and baking powder into a mixing bowl. Heat the margarine, sugar and syrup gently in a saucepan until the mixture has melted. Do not overheat. Pour this into the flour and bind together with a wooden spoon, adding the egg and enough milk to make a dough. Knead on a floured surface until it is soft but firm enough to roll out. Divide in half. Roll out one half of the dough into a rectangle approximately 5 in by 10 in (13 cm by 25 cm) and place on a greased baking tray. Divide the other piece in half and roll each out to a square 5 in by 5 in (13 cm by 13 cm). Place these on a greased baking tray (you may need two). Bake in the centre of the oven at 180°C (350°F, gas mark 4) for 15 minutes or until golden brown. Cool on a wire rack.

Youth track

The plight of the homeless and of refugees will make a thought-provoking focus to this festival. You might like to investigate local homelessness charities and also find out about the global refugee situation. You could consider raising support for a chosen charity. One method is to have a sponsored 'sleep out' and this is an annual event in our churchyard. Make sure that you invite plenty of adults too!

Recipes

Because of the harvest theme, food should be abundant at Sukkot. Fruit and nuts are especially plentiful. There is a tradition of serving 'one pot' suppers, which are easy to carry out to the sukkah, and it is also traditional to serve stuffed foods.

Among Eastern Europeans this would be stuffed cabbage leaves, whereas Sephardi Jews would use vine leaves.

Red Cabbage

This is a traditional Sukkot dish from Russia and Poland, and again follows a sweet and sour theme. It freezes well, so I usually make it in large quantities and freeze in family-sized portions.

1 red cabbage (1½ – 2 lbs)
2 onions
1 large cooking apple
1 bay leaf
4 cloves
1 dessertspoon cranberries or other red berries
2 tablespoons vinegar
1 tablespoon lemon juice
2 tablespoons kosher wine (or sweet sherry)
½ pt boiling water
1 tablespoon sugar
1 tablespoon olive or other oil

Finely slice the onion and apple. Sauté in oil. Slice the cabbage thinly (a food processor is best for this) and put in a large casserole dish. Add all the other ingredients, mix well and cook at 180°C (350°F, gas mark 4) for 1 – 1½ hours.

Apple Kreplach

Kreplach are a kind of Jewish ravioli or filled pastry. They are associated with beating, possibly because of the amount of rolling out needed to make really traditional Kreplach dough. For this reason they are eaten on the eve of Yom Kippur (with meat filling) when men traditionally beat their breasts; on the last day of Sukkot (with fruit filling) when the willow are beaten; and at Purim (with cheese filling) when Haman's name is beaten out. Cheese Kreplach are also eaten at Shavuot.

This is my own version of Apple Kreplach, which I devised after many unsuccessful attempts at making Apple Strudel!

1 packet frozen filo pastry
2 oz (55 g) butter
1 lb (450 g) cooking apples
2 oz (55 g) cake crumbs
2 oz (55 g) sultanas
2 oz (55 g) sugar
1 lemon
1 teaspoon cinnamon
1 beaten egg

Prepare filo pastry following the instructions on the packet (it is usually advised to use about three sheets that are brushed with butter as they are laid on top of each other). Finely grate the rind of the lemon and squeeze half the juice into a bowl. Add the sultanas, sugar and cinnamon. Finely chop the apple and combine with the other ingredients. Cut the pastry into 3 in (8 cm) squares. Dust some cake crumbs onto the pastry squares, then place a spoonful of filling in the centre of each and brush the edges with beaten egg. Fold over to make triangles and seal edges firmly. Use any leftover egg to glaze the pastry. Place on a lightly greased baking sheet and bake in a hot oven (200°C, 400°F, gas mark 6) for about 10 minutes or until golden. Dust with icing sugar before serving.

Traditional Kreplach are boiled in water (or in chicken soup for Yom Kippur). You can use the instructions above for these, substituting a cheese blintz style filling for Purim or Shavuot, and a meat filling for Yom Kippur made of minced meat, finely chopped onion and seasoning.

Notes

1. Hareuveni, N., *Nature in Our Biblical Heritage* (Neot Kedumim: Israel,1980), pp. 69–75.
2. Jerusalem Talmud, Hai Gaon Responsum.
3. Revelation 21:23; 22:1.
4. Maidenhead Synagogue, near London, took this as their theme for a Sukkot celebration in the late 1990s.
5. Testet, B., (ed), *Harvest Roots, a resource pack for churches and groups* (Olive Press: St Albans, 1994) gives further ideas for a Christian celebration of Sukkot.

Chapter Seven

HANUKKAH – A FESTIVAL OF LIGHTS

'Would you like to visit Modi'in?' We had just finished lunch with a Messianic Israeli friend. We had never seen this particular town and were pleased to have the opportunity. Modi'in is about halfway between Jerusalem and Tel Aviv, on the border between Israel and the West Bank. We soon found ourselves going through a checkpoint and into some very beautiful countryside. There were scattered Arab villages and among them newer Israeli settlements. The modern city of Modi'in was not quite as I had imagined. This was Maccabee country and, although the new settlement is not on the site of the biblical one, I had still envisaged an old city like Jerusalem or Jaffa. Instead we found ourselves heading towards a futuristic town of tower blocks, plazas and walkways. Springing out of the arid countryside, I thought it would not have looked out of place as a set for a scene from Star Wars. Perhaps that is not such an inappropriate monument to the heroes behind the festival of Hanukkah.

The story of the Maccabees

The Maccabees lived in the period between the last of the books of the Old Testament and the beginning of the New. At this time the Syrian Greeks ruled Israel and there had been an increasing Hellenisation of Israeli culture. Initially this only affected the social side of people's lives, such as language, sports, dress and general lifestyle. It did not affect the Jewish religion, which was allowed to continue as before. However, the country gradually became more and more Hellenised, and many 'modern' Greek-orientated Jews saw their more traditional compatriots and their religion as out of date. When Antiochus Epiphanes became king of the region in 175 BC, tolerance ended and he imposed the Greek religion throughout his kingdom. He forbade the keeping of Shabbat and the Jewish law, including kosher rules and circumcision. To celebrate a pagan holiday, he desecrated the Temple by sacrificing a pig on the altar and sprinkling its blood in the Holy of Holies. Soldiers went throughout the land and forced Jewish priests to make similar sacrifices, eat pork and worship idols. In the books of the Maccabees, where this period is recorded in the Apocrypha, there are accounts of heroic martyrdom from those who stood firm. The most famous is of a widow, traditionally called Hannah, who had seven sons (2 Maccabees 7). Each in turn was asked to bow down and eat forbidden pork, and as each refused they were horribly murdered. Finally Hannah herself was also challenged and she too died for her faith.

Eventually the soldiers came to the town of Modi'in and commanded the leading priest, Mattathias, to sacrifice a pig on a pagan altar. He refused, and, when another Jew came forward to perform the act, Mattathias drew his sword and killed both him and the king's officer. He then made the proclamation 'Follow me all who are zealous for the law and stand by the covenant!' (1 Maccabees 2:27, REV) and left for the hills with his five sons, John, Simeon, Judah Maccabee, Eleazar and Jonathan. Mattathias knew he was too old to lead the people and so he appointed Simeon to be the overall leader and Judah Maccabee to be the military commander. The nickname 'Maccabee' may have come from his military strength and be derived from the Hebrew word for hammer; or it may be an acrostic for their battle cry: 'Mi Kamoha Ba'alim Adonai' (Who is like you among the gods, O Lord).[1] As more people came out to the hills to join them, these 'Maccabees' began to plan a revolt against Greek rule. Greek troops were mobilised in Jerusalem and marched out to fight the rebels. The Maccabees were vastly outnumbered and were not trained as soldiers, but Judah Maccabee was a great tactical leader and led what would today be called a guerrilla campaign. Moreover, the Maccabees put their trust in God, and, in 164 BC, after a three–year campaign, they miraculously pushed the Greek army back to Syria. Although the campaign still continued for some years, they had gained control of much of Judea and were able to ride triumphantly into Jerusalem. There they found the Temple horribly desecrated and the statue of Zeus within the Holy Place. Removing the abominations and the altar stones, which had been defiled, they took new unhewn stones and built a new altar. They made new sacred vessels and repaired the Menorah and other Temple objects. On 25 Kislev (in December), they were ready to rededicate the Temple, exactly one year after it had been desecrated. Hanukkah is Hebrew for dedication.

Previous dedications, by Solomon and Nehemiah, had been during the feast of Sukkot. The Maccabees had been unable to celebrate Sukkot fully while they had been fugitives and so this first Hanukkah took on many of the Sukkot rituals: palm branches were waved; the Menorah was re-lit and torches were brought into the Temple area. They sang the Hallel Psalms and the festival was kept for eight days.

The miracle of the oil

There is a legend in the Talmud that, when the Maccabees rededicated the Temple, they wanted to re-light the Temple Menorah but could not find any purified oil. Eventually, a single jar was found still bearing the High Priest's seal. This was enough to fuel the Menorah for one day. Even though it would take eight days for fresh oil to be procured, it was decided to light the Menorah immediately. Miraculously, the Menorah stayed alight for the eight days required to produce more oil.

Judith and Holofernes

This is another story found in the Apocrypha. Judith was a beautiful widow from a town called Bethulia. When an army led by General Holofernes besieged this town, Judith went to her city elders with a plan. With their agreement she left the city and went to see the general. He was overcome with her beauty and took her into his camp. Legend has it that after several days she prepared a meal for him of very salty cheese. Holofernes drank too much wine during the meal and fell asleep drunk. Once they were alone, Judith cut off his head and returned to her besieged city. The next day the Jews prepared to go out and fight their attackers. The besieging army, finding their general dead, fled in panic and the Jewish people were safe.

Jesus and Hanukkah

Surprisingly, the earliest historical source for this festival using the name Hanukkah or Dedication is in the New Testament. In John 10, we find an incident recorded when Jesus clashed with local Judeans in the outer courts of the Temple at the feast of Hanukkah. An understanding of the festival makes the passage much clearer:

> Then came the Feast of Dedication at Jerusalem. It was winter, and Jesus was in the Temple area walking in Solomon's Colonnade. The Jews gathered around him, saying, 'How long will you keep us in suspense? If you are the Messiah would you tell us plainly.' (John 10:22–24)

For many Jews, Hanukkah was a time when they especially hoped to find freedom from the Romans. They saw the Messiah as someone who would be similar to Judah Maccabee and were looking to Jesus to fulfil this role. Instead Jesus spoke about eternal life, of his sheep in another fold, and of his relationship with God. For people looking for a military solution to their oppression, conflict with Jesus was inevitable.

A hint of this desire for a King Messiah can also be found in the Palm Sunday story. Palm branches were waved at the first Hanukkah as the people celebrated the victory of Judah Maccabee. The palm branches of Jesus' final entrance into Jerusalem encapsulated the hope of the people that he, like Judah Maccabee, would lead the people to freedom. Although there were some who understood, many were not prepared for a Messiah who had come to suffer and die for his people and bring them new life through his resurrection.

Hanukkah in later Judaism

The tradition for lighting lamps had developed by the first century AD and the Festival of Lights is the name used for the festival in other sources at this period. One reason may have been the diplomatic problem of celebrating freedom from the Greeks when under the rule of another empire, the Romans. Also, the Maccabees founded the dynasty of the Hasmoneans, who were Sadducees, and so would not have been popular with the Pharisees. The Hanukkah lights enabled the rabbis to focus the festival on a religious theme.

For most of later Jewish history this has been the focus of Hanukkah. In the Middle Ages the theme of martyrdom for the Jewish faith grew in significance. The story of Hannah and her sons, and also that of Judith and Holofernes, became popular. These were to encourage Jewish people to stand firm in their faith against persecution. The tradition of playing with a dreidel or spinning top also became prevalent. It is thought

that, during times
people were studyi
the scroll was whisk
simply playing a g
ters on the top, N
Hayah Sham', or '

With the rise of
itary aspect of the fes
the military theme re
larly held at Modi'in, a
other parts of Israel and be
tury, especially in America, t
of Jewish Christmas. The old
'Hanukkah gelt', has been develo
giving tradition, and the Hanukka
Christmas tree as a focus for the festival.

Making the link

There is currently quite a debate among Christians sensitive to Jewish festivals over whether it might be better to celebrate Hanukkah rather than the now over–commercialised Christmas. I celebrate Christmas but I also enjoy lighting the Hanukkah lights. The festival usually comes during Advent and for me the lights are a symbol of the light of the Messiah who is coming into the world. There are nine candles on a Hanukkah Menorah, which is correctly called a Hanukkiah. Eight of these are for each day of the festival and the ninth is called the 'Shamash' or Servant. This candle is the only one that is lit by a match and is used to light all the other candles. I see in the Shamash a symbol of the servant ministry of Jesus, and our call to follow him as servants of others.

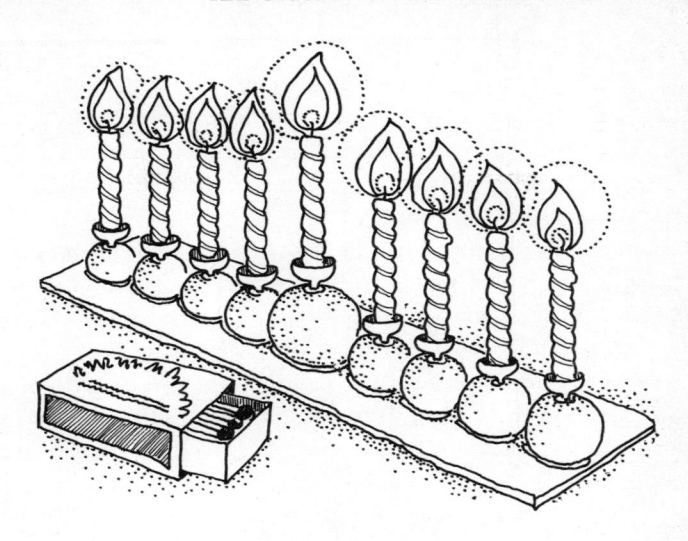

Preparing for Hanukkah

Making a Hanukkiah

You will need:

A pack of children's modelling clay
44 cake candles
9 cake candle holders
A piece of white card, 10 in (25 cm) × 2 in (5 cm), or a chopping board

Roll a piece of children's modelling clay in your hand to make a ball 1 in (2½ cm) diameter. Make seven other balls of this size in assorted colours. Roll a larger piece of modelling clay in your hand to make a ball 1½ in (4 cm) diameter – this will hold the servant candle.

Measure to find the middle spot on the piece of card and push the larger ball firmly onto the card at this spot. Working outwards from the centre ball, position four other balls in a row on either side of your middle ball of modelling clay. Then position your candle holders. The servant candle will be on the middle larger ball – simply stick it into the top. Position the others on the ball of modelling clay on either side.

You are now ready to place some candles and light your Hanukkiah. Light as follows:

First night: place one candle for the Shamash on the middle candle holder and one candle to the far right. Light the Shamash with a match and then use the Shamash to light the first candle.

Second night: place two candles on the right of the Hanukkiah and a Shamash in the middle. Light the Shamash with a match and then use the Shamash to light the other two candles – lighting the one furthest to the left first.

Third and following nights: repeat the procedure, adding a candle every night.

Youth track

Make a list of the famous women in the Bible. What roles did they take and what made their lives significant? Can you list any well-known Christian and Jewish women today? How do they compare with their biblical counterparts and what conclusions can we draw from the comparison?

Recipes

Hanukkah is often jokingly called the heart attack festival. This is because all the traditional foods, such as latkes and cheese pancakes contain oil or cheese. Modern American dishes include doughnuts and savoury dishes such as the cheesecake below.

Non-Kosher Latkes

Latkes are not easy to find ready-made outside Jewish areas. The mixture is made of grated potato and onion. This is mixed with flour and egg, formed into cakes, and deep-fried. Since I do not live near Jewish shops, or possess a deep fat fryer, I cheat! Frozen potato waffles make a reasonable substitute. For the full Hanukkah effect they should be served with sour cream and apple sauce. Your children will either love it or hate it!

Savoury Spinach Cheesecake

This is my own recipe for Hanukkah. It is a mildly salty (as opposed to a sweet) cheesecake. It can be served with any winter vegetables and is delicious hot or cold. Check to see if the cottage cheese is salted or not – if it is, do not add any more.

For 4 people

Base

4 oz (115 g) oats
1 oz (30 g) sunflower seeds
A pinch of garlic powder
2 oz (50 g) melted butter

Top

A beaten egg
10 oz (280 g) frozen chopped spinach
1 crushed garlic clove
1 small onion, chopped
1¼ lb (550 g) cottage cheese
pepper to season
1 oz (30 g) grated cheddar

Defrost the spinach and drain off excess liquid. Lightly grease a baking dish 8 in by 6 in (21 cm by 16 cm). Mix the base ingredients together and then press down into the bottom of the dish. Pre-heat the oven to 180°C (350°F, gas mark 4) and bake in the oven for 20 minutes while you make the topping.

Sweat the onion and garlic lightly in a pan and add the spinach to warm through, remove from the heat and mix in the cheese and pepper. Beat the egg in a large bowl and gently fold in the mixed ingredients. Meanwhile, remove the base from the oven and allow to cool just slightly. Place the topping onto the base, sprinkle the grated cheese on the very top and bake for about 50 minutes or until the cake is set and the top is melted and golden.

Note

1. Renburg, D. F., *The complete family guide to Jewish holidays* (Robson Books: London, 1987), p. 90.

Chapter Eight

TU B'SHVAT – CARE FOR CREATION

Most people take photographs when they visit Israel. Often they are surprised by the beauty of the countryside and want to take away a record of the holy sites they have visited. I had not known my husband long before I discovered that, as a plant biologist, his photo collection was rather different. On our first trip to the Church of the Beatitudes instead of photographing the church, I found him wandering off in the other direction going after a 'very interesting' irrigation scheme. On our latest visit, we screeched to a halt on the track leading up to the church to enable him to photograph a large yellow weed that is one of Israel's current ecological problems. The quizzical looks from people on the tour buses going past made it clear that teaching about weeds was not on the average tour itinerary.

Knowing our natural history interests, we were once asked by Monarch Publishers if we had a photograph of a fig tree. We did not have a picture but were about to lead a Shoresh tour of Israel and so this seemed quite achievable.[1] It did not take us long to discover why we had no photographs – they are not the most photogenic of trees. They generally form a large mound shape, giving them an unkempt and rather shaggy look. Still we kept trying to find a pretty fig tree and before long had big figs and little figs, photographs of the leaves and of the fruit. On a later winter trip we just had to photograph the small male figs, which are home for a special insect grub that emerges as a wasp in the spring to fertilise the flowers. When our slides dropped through the post, however, we had to admit that none of the trees were really attractive. Now when we go walking in Israel, whenever we smell the sweet sickly smell of the fig we remember our attempts and have to resist the temptation of trying again! The fig is the oldest tree recorded by name in the Hebrew Bible and one of the seven fruits that the Israelites were commanded to offer up at the Temple in Jerusalem.[2]

Tu b'Shvat is a festival dedicated to Israel's trees. Its roots go back to the book of Leviticus, though it only became a festival in the post biblical period.

The origins of Tu b'Shvat

Tu b'Shvat is a New Year for trees. This might seem a strange concept for anyone living outside the Levitical law, but it has a very practical function. There are a number of commandments in the Torah concerning trees. The Israelites were forbidden to eat the fruit of a new tree for three years after it had been planted. On the fourth year the fruit had to be given as a praise offering, and only on the fifth year might the fruit be eaten (Leviticus 19:23–25). Since trees produce fruit at different times and have quite a long process leading up to fruit formation, a problem arose in determining in which year the fruit of the tree originated. It was therefore decided that a date should be set to mark a change of year for trees. In Israel the rains come in the winter and are mostly finished by mid-February. Deciduous trees drop their leaves in winter and very little sap is drawn up through the plant. As spring approaches, the sap begins to flow again and new growth starts. The sages decided that the time when the rain stopped and sap began to flow was the point when the New Year began for trees. There was some discussion as to the exact date but it was eventually set at 15 Shvat, which usually occurs in February. If you were in the fourth year after planting a new tree and looking to the fifth, any fruit that started to form before 15 Shvat was holy and should be offered to God, but any starting to form after that date was your own and could be eaten.

It was also important for tithing. A tenth of each year's produce had to be given to the priests. Tu b'Shvat provided the date when the next year's crop began. If your tree blossomed before then, even though the fruit had not formed, it counted in last year's tithe.

How Tu b'Shvat developed

Tu b'Shvat is first mentioned in the second century AD in the Mishnah, but all the traditions for this festival are late, mostly coming from the Middle Ages onward. In Eastern Europe it became a custom to eat fifteen different kinds of fruit and to try, if possible, to have some dried ones from Israel. This was often carob as they survived well on the long journey. Almonds were seen as especially linked to this festival, as they are the first tree to blossom in Israel and this frequently coincided with Tu b'Shvat. Psalm 104 was recited, which emphasises God as creator.

In the sixteenth century in Israel, the kabbalistic Jews of Safed developed an elaborate service called a Tu b'Shvat Seder. Modelled on a Passover meal, it had its own special traditions. They noticed that different colour flowers predominated during different seasons in the Holy Land and wove these colours into their celebration of the changing seasons.

The Tu b'Shvat Seder

We were once invited to a Messianic Tu b'Shvat Seder. It was obviously going to be an artistic event because we were asked to bring a poem, an object or a thought about God and the natural world, and it was to be held in a Bedouin tent. We went along aware that we were fairly well off the main highway of evangelical Christianity (to say the least), but hoping to find out what Judaism could teach us about a deeper appreciation of nature.

We arrived to find a Middle Eastern feast of fruits laid out for us in the centre of the tent. The evening was divided into four sections and each had its own course of fruit or nuts and each had a glass of wine as in a Passover Seder. The four cups were to represent the different seasons. The first was of white wine and was for winter and the physical world. We thought about our problem of being hard-hearted towards nature and not realising the problems around us. For this course we ate fruit with a hard outer shell such as almonds and pomegranates.

For the second course we added a little red wine to our white and found ourselves in spring and the realm of feelings and emotions. One or two people read poems about how vulnerable nature is and how it has been violated. For this course we had fruit with a soft outside and a hard centre, such as dates, cherries and rather delicious avocado soup. A little more red wine was added again for summer and the world of the intellect. What can we do to behave responsibly towards creation? Here we tried fruit that was entirely edible such as figs, grapes or pears.

Finally our glass was pure red wine and the autumn season of the spiritual realm. This is when the rain comes in Israel, which is seen as a sign of God's blessing and a symbol of his Holy Spirit. We cannot act in our own strength, but need to realise that we are both stewards of the earth, and ourselves created by God. This could not be represented by fruit but by our openness to deepen our relationship with him.

Late at night, after much fruit, wine, poetry and thought-provoking contributions, we left the Bedouin tent to return home to our rather more regular Christianity, enriched with a deeper sense of God's concern for his creation.[3]

Sabbath rest

A theme in many modern Tu b'Shvat celebrations is the Sabbatical year commanded in Leviticus 25. The Israelites were commanded to give the land a rest every seventh year. They were allowed to eat anything that grew naturally, but not to plough, plant or systematically harvest crops. In this way the land could regenerate itself and produce more abundantly in the other six years. Apart from being a good early example of using fallow years in agriculture, the purpose of the sabbatical year was to teach the Israelites that they did not own the land. This was holy and belonged to God, who lent it to them. Consequently they should treat it with respect. When the people of God were carried off into exile for disobedience, this was mentioned. Farmers had not been abiding by the Sabbatical year rule and so God had intervened: 'The land enjoyed its Sabbath rests, all the time of its desolation it rested, until the seventy years (of exile) were completed' (2 Chronicles 36:21).

Modern customs

When Jewish people first returned in numbers to Palestine in the nineteenth century, many pioneers started new farms. Initially the sabbatical laws were not enforced by the rabbinical authorities, who realised that these farmers were barely surviving. As the land became more prosperous the sabbatical year was reintroduced, and there is now a distinction between those religious farms and kibbutzim who do abide by them and those who are secular and do not. The first sabbatical year in the new State of Israel was in 1952, and they have occurred every seven years since.

Planting trees in Israel

In the New Testament period it was traditional to plant a tree when a child was born: a cedar was planted that would grow strong and tall, for a boy; and a cypress that is fragrant and elegant, for a girl. When the child grew up and married, the wood from their tree was used to make the huppah or wedding canopy.[4]

A modern tradition that was started by the early Zionist pioneers was to plant a tree on Tu b'Shvat. When Napoleon retreated from the Holy Land in 1798 he literally burned the land behind him. The result was terrible ecological devastation. There was little recovery in the nineteenth century because of a tax on trees. With the establishment of Israel, funds were started so that Jewish people in the Diaspora could contribute to the reafforestation of the land. This campaign still continues and many new forests have been planted.

Making the link

Tu b'Shvat was not known as a festival during biblical times, though it is based on the teaching of the Bible concerning our relationship to the land and its produce. Jesus was familiar with the tithing of crops and sabbatical years. He would probably have been aware of the debate over the exact date when one year finished and another started and, in Luke 11:42, he criticised the Pharisees for being exact with the details of tithing but not the fundamentals of loving respect for God and other people. Jesus maintains that both are important.

It is beyond the scope of this chapter to give a full appreciation of the teaching in the Bible concerning nature. There are principles Christians can learn from this Jewish ecological festival. First and foremost, that the earth and its natural life are not our possession but have been placed in our care by God. It is our responsibility to use trees and other natural resources conscientiously. The principle of tithing is a good one, as is that of setting aside our first and best fruits for God. We should also realise that, as we have benefited from previous generations in, for example, the planting of fruit trees, we in turn should provide for those coming after us. There is a lovely verse in Deuteronomy that sums up this respectful attitude:

> When you lay siege to a city for a long time, fighting against it to capture it, do not destroy its trees by putting an axe to them, because you can eat their fruit. Do not cut them down. Are the trees of the field people, that you should besiege them? (Deuteronomy 20:19)

For Christians, Tu b'Shvat may not be so much a festival to be celebrated as a principle to remember.

Celebrating creation

Imagine a world without trees! Maybe this is the year to decide to plant a tree. If you do not have a garden big enough and if your church is not in need of further forestation, you might find that an environmental charity could plant one for you or provide a location. If you have room for a garden tree, consider a fruit-bearing one. It might be many years before it bears fruit, but this is one way in which you can provide for future generations.

Grow your own

A good activity for children is to grow a tree seedling. One of the best is an avocado stone. These now grow in Israel as an introduced crop. Make sure that the sharp end is facing upwards, then stick three wooden cocktail sticks around the middle of your avocado stone, resembling arms sticking out. Fill an old glass beaker with water almost to the top and then balance your avocado stone over it. It will take several weeks to germinate, and you will need to top up the water. Once the top begins to shoot and some roots appear, you can transfer it to some potting compost and grow it as a house plant.

Youth track

If you live near any woodland, try to find something out about its history. Has it decreased or increased in size over the last fifty years? Who manages it? You may have the opportunity to help! If you live right in the city, map the trees in your local area. Are there some parts with more trees than others? Do trees make a city more attractive?

Food for Tu b'Shvat

It is a good exercise to try to make up a meal with only the produce of trees. For example, you could have toasted bananas with flaked almonds to start, followed by a nut loaf, accompanied by a salad made up of avocados, olives, apples, pineapples and oranges. Serve with a pepper, lemon and olive oil dressing. Dessert might be various dried fruits such as dates, figs and raisins. End with coffee.

Almond Cookies

These Persian style biscuits are appropriate because almond trees often flower at Tu b'Shvat.

6 oz (140 g) plain flour
5 oz (140 g) ground almonds
3 oz (85 g) butter
4 cardamon pods.
3 oz (85 g) caster sugar
1 beaten egg
1 teaspoon baking powder.

Rub the fat into the flour and then rub in the ground almonds and combine with the sugar and baking powder. Grind the seeds from the cardamon pods and mix in. Add about ¾ of the egg and combine to make a dough. Roll this out and cut into 2½ in (6 cm) circles with a pastry cutter. Brush with the remainder of the egg, place on a lightly greased baking tray and bake for 20 to 25 minutes in a warm oven, 190°C (375°F, gas mark 5). Cool on a wire rack.

Notes

1. Shoresh run study tours of Israel that especially highlight the Jewish roots to the Christian faith. 'Shoresh' is the Hebrew word for 'root'.
2. Genesis 3:7; Deuteronomy 8:8.
3. I am grateful to the organiser of the Seder, H. Clouts, for allowing me to use her notes for this section.
4. Renburg, D. F., *The complete family guide to Jewish holidays* (Robson Books: London, 1987), p. 109.

Chapter Nine

PURIM – DELIVERED FROM OUR ENEMIES

Imagine an early spring afternoon in West Jerusalem. Children are coming out of school, not in ordinary clothes but in fancy dress costume. They are wearing masks and some are carrying noisy rattles. They appear to have had a party, not a serious school day! This is Purim, and for children it is possibly the most fun-filled festival in the Jewish religious calendar. It celebrates one of the great Jewish heroines of the Hebrew Bible, Queen Esther. Her story is told on the evening that the festival begins and her bravery is celebrated in numerous 'Purim plays', in schools and homes throughout Israel.

The origins of Purim

Esther was a Jewish woman who eventually became a queen. She was an orphan and had been brought up by her older cousin, Mordecai. The book of Esther begins with the story of how the king divorced his first wife for disobedience and then sent his officials on a search for a perfect queen. Esther became one of the candidates. Her beauty and modesty won the heart of the king and the loyalty of his officials. This orphan girl found herself unexpectedly made Queen of Persia. After she entered the king's household in Susa, Mordecai would go to the palace gates to find out how she was. One day he heard a plot to kill the king. He told Esther, who was able to prevent the plot. Mordecai's loyalty was recorded in the palace records.

In many stories there is a wicked person who is eventually defeated. In this book it is Haman, the king's top adviser. Haman decreed that everyone should bow to him. Everyone did bar one, Mordecai, because he would only bow down to the one true God. Haman became very angry and, when he discovered that Mordecai was Jewish, he decided to kill Mordecai and all the other Jews with him. He could not decide which day to do it, so he threw lots. This is why the Feast of Esther is called Purim, which is Hebrew for 'lots'. The lot fell on the thirteenth day of the month of Adar. When Mordecai heard about this, he challenged Esther to approach the king to save her people. At first she was reluctant, because approaching the king without an audience could be punished by death. Mordecai sent a second message to Esther that, if she would not help, God would bring deliverance by another method but she would suffer for her unwillingness to help. This time Esther agreed. She asked that the whole Jewish community fast for three days and nights, and promised that she and her household would do the same. Afterwards she would approach the king.

Haman did not know Esther was Jewish, or a relative of Mordecai, and so she could have probably saved herself by remaining silent. Instead, after prayer and fasting, she approached the king and invited him to a banquet along with Haman. After the banquet, the king could not sleep. He decided that there must be something not in order with his kingdom. He ordered a servant to look up the records and discovered that a man called Mordecai had never been rewarded for uncovering a serious plot against him.

The next day Haman boasted about his position to his family and friends: 'Even Queen Esther honours me above all the other king's officials.' The one cloud on his horizon was Mordecai. He decided to build a gallows and hang Mordecai on it. He went to the palace and was ushered into the presence of the king. The king asked Haman what he should do for the man he wished to honour. Haman, thinking the king meant him, suggested that he should be given a royal robe and ride the king's horse with someone beside him saying that this is the man the king delights to honour. The king agreed but asked that Haman do this for Mordecai! Haman was mortified. That night there was another banquet. This time Esther told the king she was Jewish, the cousin of Mordecai, and that they and all their people were about to be murdered on Haman's orders. The king was furious and ordered that Haman instead be killed on the very gallows he had built for Mordecai. Mordecai was then made chief adviser to the king, and the Jewish people were saved. On the fourteenth of Adar there was a great celebration among Esther's people. Mordecai sent out an edict to all the Jewish communities to celebrate Purim each year as a day when God gave deliverance from their enemies.

How Purim developed as a festival

Knowing a little of Jewish history we can understand why this biblical story of the beautiful and heroic queen, guided by her wise cousin, has remained so popular. It appears to have begun to be celebrated during the period of the Second Temple. This was a time of subjection to ruling empires and is also the period that Hanukkah became established. The first written record of Purim is in 2 Maccabees 15:36 where it is described as Mordecai's Day and linked to victory over a Syrian general, Nicanor. By the second century AD, Purim, described as the 'Feast of Esther', was significant enough to justify a tractate in the Mishnah. This tractate is known as 'Megillah' which is the Hebrew word for 'scroll'. It contains instructions for the reading of the book of Esther, which is often known simply as 'The Megillah'.

The reading of the scroll has remained the central element of the festival through the centuries and it is read both on the day of Purim and on the evening before. It was forbidden for any illustrations to be added to the scrolls of any other book in the Bible, but an exception was made for the Megillah because there is no direct mention of God in the book. Esther scrolls are frequently highly decorated. It also became traditional for children to have rattles and other noisemakers, so that when the name of Haman was mentioned they would try to drown it out with their noise! This encapsulates both the fun of Purim and also the cuttingly serious side to the day.

Purim pranks

Purim became known as a day for fun, foolishness and practical jokes. In the Middle Ages a tradition started in which a comic figure in the community was picked to be a 'Purim Rabbi' who reigned over humorous anarchy and would give a totally frivolous but often brilliant sermon on the Bible.[1] There was even a parody written of the Talmud, where the main 'law' was to drink lots of wine and be as happy as possible! In Italy, Jewish communities started to devise Purim plays and this started the tradition of dressing up, which is so popular for children's parties today.

Purim and persecution

Beneath the merriment, the theme of persecution is always near the surface. Purim counterbalances the harsh reality of persecution experienced by Jewish communities. One friend of mine, whose family escaped Nazi Germany, told me that as a child he would stamp his feet to blot out the name of

Haman. On the sole of one shoe he would put the name 'Haman' and on the sole of the other shoe he wrote the name 'Hitler'. There are accounts of communities who had their own individual 'Purims' to celebrate their deliverance from a particular persecution. In recent history, Israelis saw it as significant that the 1991 Gulf War ended on this festival.

Other traditions

The other traditions at Purim are to eat a festive meal, to give gifts, especially of food, and to give alms to the poor. This is in obedience to the original instructions of Mordecai recorded in Esther 9:22: 'He wrote to them to observe the days as days of feasting and joy and giving of presents of food to one another and gifts to the poor.'

Purim is a minor holiday where work is still permitted. To prevent too much work squeezing out the enjoyment of the festival, the rabbis decided that the festive meal should be eaten during the day rather than in the evening. So it is normally eaten in the afternoon and is traditionally accompanied by a generous amount of wine. The Talmud suggests reaching a point when you are unable to tell the difference between the name of Haman and the name of Mordecai! This is thought to be because overindulgence punctuates the Esther story. Many Jewish communities were also at the mercy of rulers who lived extravagant lifestyles and could wipe them out on a whim. So perhaps for just a day, these communities decided to live the high life and forget their precarious position.

Nothing is quite as it seems in Purim. The name of God is never mentioned in the book of Esther but his unseen hand is assumed to be directing events. Esther hid her identity ('Esther' derives from a word meaning 'to conceal'), and Haman believed that he was the one to be honoured, but was in fact humiliated. So in this festival we enter into a topsy-turvy world where the fool becomes the rabbi and the children hide their identity with masks and fancy dress. Fun is made of both sacred books and rabbinic teachers that are held in such high esteem during the rest of the year.

Making the link

There is no reference to Purim in the New Testament and it was also the only Book of the Hebrew Bible not to be found in the Dead Sea Scrolls, although the evidence does suggest that it was known in this period. The basic story of the willingness of one person to risk her life for the sake of her people has a redemptive theme.

There are similarities with the Mardi Gras carnival festivities of European Christian communities. The noise, the merry-making, the fancy dress and even the buffoon are all features of pre-Lent carnivals among Christians.[2] There is no doubt that these traditions developed together in Europe and influenced each other. God created both laughter and humour and Christians unused to carnival traditions may learn from both Purim and Mardi Gras the value of sometimes being frivolous rather than always taking ourselves terribly seriously!

The other side of Purim – gaiety in the face of grim persecution – is entirely Jewish. Christians can enter into the fun and frivolity of this day, but should not forget that the story of prayer and bravery overcoming hatred and murderous intent did not end at Susa.

Have a Purim party!

Purim has great party ideas for children. There are plenty of opportunities for making masks and fancy dress clothes and it can also be fun to make noisemakers. It is a good time to teach about giving to others. Try making up small baskets of special food to take to friends or older relatives.

Making noisemakers

You will need:

A jam jar with a lid
Dried pulse vegetables such as chickpeas
Bright coloured paper
Sticky tape.

This is very simple and is good for small children. Fill your jam jar ¼ full with dried pulses. Screw the lid on firmly. Cut a piece of paper to wrap round your jar and stick this in place. You are now ready to shake your noisemaker and experiment with sounds. Different sized pulses will make different noises, so if you can make several you can build up a percussion orchestra!

Purim masks

You will need:
Thin white card
Fine string
Crayons.

Draw out the shape of a 'highwayman' style mask. Make holes large enough for your eyes and a small hole at either end for the string. Decorate your mask with crayons. Cut two lengths of string of the right length to fit the mask onto your head. Thread these through the smaller holes and tie securely. You are now ready to try out your mask.

Youth track

The word 'anti-Semitism' was coined in the last century to describe the persecution of Jewish people. If the word is relatively recent, the reality is very old indeed and goes right back to biblical times. Use your local library to find out about the history of anti-Semitism. What have been the worst periods of history for Jewish people? Have Christians been involved in anti-Semitism? Does it still happen today and what can we do to help eradicate it?

Recipes

The tradition of giving food to others has created a festival full of delicious sweet foods. If Hanukkah is the heart attack festival this is probably the one to keep quiet about to your dentist. Poppy seeds are traditional at Purim time. This is because the Yiddish and German words for 'poppy seed' sound very similar to the name Haman. Most traditional are pastries filled with poppy seeds called Hamantashen. These resemble three-cornered hats and are sometimes called Haman's ears or Haman's pockets.

Hamantashen

Pastry

5 oz (140 g) plain flour
3 oz (85 g) butter
5 oz (140 g) ground almonds
1 oz (30 g) caster sugar
1 beaten egg

Filling

1 oz (28 g) poppy seeds
2 tablespoons honey
½ tablespoon water
1 oz (28 g) currants
1 oz (28 g) chopped almonds
1 dessertspoon sherry (optional)

To serve

Caster sugar
Hundreds and thousands

Rub the fat into the flour and then rub in the ground almonds and combine with the sugar. Add enough egg (about half) to make a cohesive, but not wet, pastry. Place in a covered bowl and allow to cool in the refrigerator while you make up the filling. Combine all the filling ingredients in a small saucepan and simmer until the mixture has thickened. Allow to cool. Roll the pastry out and cut into 3 in (8 cm) circles with a pastry cutter. Put a level teaspoon of the filling onto each of the rounds and draw up the sides of each to make a three-cornered hat shape. Make sure the pastry is squeezed together enough to prevent the filling leaking out and try not to over-fill. Brush with the remainder of the egg, place on a lightly greased baking tray and bake for 20 to 25 minutes in a warm oven, 190°C (375°F, gas mark 5). Cool on a wire rack and dust with caster sugar and hundreds and thousands.

Lemon and poppy seed cake

This cake sounds complicated but is really very easy.
2 oz (70 g) poppy seeds
2 tablespoons honey
2 tablespoons water
4 oz (115 g) butter, softened
4 oz (115 g) sugar
2 eggs
Grated peel and juice of one large lemon
6 fl oz (170 ml) plain yoghurt
8 oz (220 g) plain flour
1 teaspoon bicarbonate of soda
1 teaspoon baking powder
½ teaspoon salt

First pour the honey and water into a saucepan and add the poppy seeds. Heat for a few minutes until all the seeds are moistened. Allow to cool then add the lemon juice. Cream the butter and sugar then beat in the eggs, the yoghurt and the lemon peel. Mix in the seed mixture. Fold in the flour, bicarbonate of soda, baking powder and salt. Divide between two lightly greased sponge tins and bake in a warm oven, 190°C (375°F, gas mark 5) for about 30 minutes or until a skewer comes out clean when thrust into the cake. Turn out and cool on a wire rack.

Filling

4 oz (110 g) cream cheese
1 oz (30 g) icing sugar
A few drops of vanilla essence

Beat the cheese and sugar together and then mix in the vanilla essence. Spread on the base of one of the sponges and place the other on top. Lightly dust the top of the cake with icing sugar before serving.

Notes

1. Strassfeld, M., *The Jewish holidays, A Guide and Commentary* (Harper and Row: New York, 1985), p.191.
2. Schauss, H., *The Jewish festivals* (Jewish Chronicle Publications: London, 1986), pp. 268–270.

Chapter Ten

SABBATH – REST AND PRAYER WITH THE FAMILY

One year we spent a Shabbat at a kibbutz guest house. We had just arrived in Israel and the weather was perfect as we had a Friday evening pre-dinner stroll around our kibbutz in the beautiful Judean hills.

Many Orthodox families had been arriving for the weekend, and, when we went into the dining room, we expected something special for Shabbat. Sure enough, there was a table full of candles which women lit as they came in, and the dining tables were laid out with kosher wine and rich challah Sabbath bread. We were early, and the room was fairly empty, despite the large number of candles lit. We were surprised that those present did not say blessings over the wine and bread – well, this was a kibbutz! We ate our meal, and, as we were about to go, there was a second influx of people, and suddenly the situation became clear. These were the religious Jews who were coming to dinner after a synagogue service. The men were wearing kippot on their heads and the women had scarves or were wearing scheitels (wigs). Out came the prayer books and then, table by table, each family or couple 'made Kiddush' – saying the traditional blessings over the wine and bread, which was dipped into salt before being eaten.

Sabbath runs from sundown on Friday until sundown on Saturday, and Friday evening, or 'Erev Shabbat', as it is known in Hebrew, is an important part of the Sabbath. The Jewish practice of counting days in this way stems from the Genesis account of Creation where the days run from evening to evening. Here we also find the origin of the Sabbath rest.

Sabbath in the Hebrew Bible

God created rest

In the beginning of Genesis we find the account of the creation of the world. The Hebrew name for Genesis is 'Bereshit' which means 'In the beginning'. God created the world and everything in it in seven days. Each day started in the evening ('And there was evening and there was morning – the first day' – Genesis 1:5). Once the heavens and the earth were created, Genesis continues:

> By the seventh day God had finished the work he had been doing; so on the seventh day he rested from all his work. And God blessed the seventh day and made it holy, because on it he rested from all the work of creating that he had done. (Genesis 2:2–3)

The English word 'Sabbath' is a direct transliteration of the Hebrew. 'Sabbath' is an intriguing word because it comes from a Hebrew root verb 'Shabbat' meaning 'to rest' but also contains echoes of the Hebrew word for seven, 'Sheva'.[1] Rabbi Jonathan Sacks explains that the rabbis believed that this seventh day of rest was also something that God created: 'After six days, what did the universe lack? It lacked rest. So when the seventh day came, rest came and the universe was complete.'[2]

We do not find the Sabbath day mentioned again in the

Bible until the book of Exodus where it is commanded as a day of rest for the Israelites. No indication is given whether it was observed as a rest day before this time. It is first outlined in Exodus 16 where the instructions are given for manna and quail. Each day there would be enough food for that day only, and if any were saved it would go bad. On the sixth day, however, the Israelites were commanded to collect a double portion, which would stay fresh for two days. In this way the Sabbath could be observed as a day of rest. Jewish people still remember the double portion of manna by placing two Sabbath loaves on the table for the eve of Shabbat.

A sign of the covenant

The culmination of the Exodus instructions for the Sabbath came in the Ten Commandments given to Moses on Mount Sinai.

> Remember the Sabbath day by keeping it holy. Six days you shall labour and do all your work, but the seventh day is a Sabbath to the Lord your God. On it you shall not do any work, neither you, nor your son or daughter, nor your manservant or maidservant, nor your animals, nor the alien within your gates. For in six days the Lord made the heavens and the earth, the sea, and all that is in them, but he rested on the seventh day. Therefore the Lord blessed the Sabbath day and made it holy. (Exodus 20:8–11)

This passage reveals the strong community element to the keeping of Sabbath, and in this it is highly humanitarian. It was not simply the head of household who should keep the Sabbath for religious purposes, but the whole household should have rest, including the servants and even extending to the animals. This continues the Genesis command to be stewards of creation.

Most importantly, it should be noted that the Israelites were commanded to *keep* the Sabbath holy, not to *make* it holy. The implication is that God created it as a holy day, and we need to honour it as such. When reflecting on the wilderness experience of the Israelites, Ezekiel saw this commandment to keep the Sabbath as a sign of God's covenant with Israel: 'I gave them my Sabbaths as a sign between us, so that they would know that I the Lord made them holy' (Ezekiel 20:12). Not only did God make the Sabbath holy, but he also made the people of God holy.

Ignoring the Sabbath

Once Sabbath became established as a command of the covenant, it also became a sign of obedience to the covenant. Inevitably this would lead to Sabbath violation and this came under judgement both of the people and of God. Ezekiel continues: 'Yet the people of Israel rebelled against me in the desert. They did not follow my decrees but rejected my laws – although the man who obeys them will live by them – and they utterly desecrated my Sabbaths' (Ezekiel 20:13).

In Numbers 15:32–36 we find the first example of Sabbath violation. An Israelite was found gathering wood on the Sabbath. They were initially not sure what to do with him, but, after seeking the Lord, they stoned him to death. This seems a very severe penalty indeed and shows the seriousness with which Sabbath was taken at that time. Once in the land, it did not seem to be taken quite so strictly and people used to travel to visit Jerusalem or to enquire of a holy man (2 Kings 4:23). In Babylon, Sabbath developed as a far stricter day of rest, but on the return from exile, Nehemiah found that in Jerusalem the Sabbath was treated as an ordinary day of trade. Both Jews and people from Tyre were bringing merchandise into the city on Shabbat to sell. Nehemiah (13:15–22) spoke against this. His solution was to close the gates of the city just before the Sabbath started and not open them again until it had ended.

Today in Jerusalem a siren sounds to announce the start of

Sabbath. For many people it is a complete day of rest and worship, but some cafes open and there are still cars on the roads. Many of the passing Orthodox Jews will shout 'Shabbas Shabbas' at the car drivers. There is tremendous tension between the very strict communities, the moderately religious and the more secular people. For most people in Israel, Saturday is their only day off work in the week. They would like to spend the day in leisure activities but many of these – such as driving to the beach, or even to a religious meeting – involve violating the Sabbath. To some extent, this mirrors the situation in the Old Testament. The prophet Isaiah considered that:

> If you keep your feet from breaking the Sabbath and from doing as you please on my holy day, if you call the Sabbath a delight and the Lord's holy day honourable, and if you honour it by not going your own way and not doing as you please or speaking idle words, then you will find your joy in the Lord. (Isaiah 58:13)

The problem throughout history has been the tension between observing the Sabbath properly but also making it truly a delight. A person's inner attitude is all-important. Amos (8:5) discovered that people were just waiting for the Sabbath to end so that they could reopen their businesses. He realised that it was not sufficient to simply keep the Sabbath outwardly, but one should also honour it inwardly. This deeper reflection on the meaning of Sabbath developed through the Second Temple period and it was one of the theological debates of Jesus' day.

Jesus and Sabbath

As Jesus came from an observant Jewish family, there is no reason to suppose that he did not take seriously the command to 'keep the Sabbath holy'. In Luke 4:16–30 there is a description of him going to synagogue in Nazareth on the Sabbath.

The major point of describing this incident is to show that Jesus was rejected in his home town, but it also gives us insight into his Sabbath practices. Going to synagogue on the Sabbath was his usual custom (v.16); indeed, it would be unheard of for an observant Jewish man of his day not to go to synagogue. A number of ancient synagogues have been discovered in Galilee, mostly dating from the first or second centuries AD. These, combined with rabbinic writings, give us some insights into synagogue worship in Jesus' day. As with the Temple in Jerusalem, synagogues in Galilee were generally orientated to the west, since an eastward orientation was associated with sun worship. At the front of the synagogue was a cupboard, or Ark, where the scrolls of the law were kept, and in the centre of the synagogue was the Bimah or reading desk.

Jesus must have been a respected person within his community because he was asked to read. Today in synagogue there is a reading each week from the Torah (Pentateuch) followed by a 'Haftorah' reading which is a reading from the Prophets selected to fit the Torah theme. During the year, the Torah is read through once systematically. There are various suggestions concerning the lectionary in Jesus' day. One common view is that there was a three-year cycle for reading the Torah and that there were also Haftorah readings. Each week the Torah reading was divided into three. The person who read the last portion of the Torah may also have read the Haftorah and then taught on the passages. If this were the case, Jesus would have been the person chosen not only to read but also to speak. The scrolls were written in Hebrew, and, as they were read, they were explained in Aramaic, sometimes drawing on the Septuagint for help in translation. This translation with explanation was known as a Targum, and would account for some scriptural quotes in the New Testament seeming to be a little different to the Old Testament verse in the same translation of the Bible. For example, the last two phrases of Luke 4:18 ('recovery of sight for the blind; to release the oppressed') are alternate meanings of the Hebrew original for the final line of Isaiah 61:1 ('and release from darkness for the prisoners'). This may have been a Targum by Jesus.

In our English translation of Luke it seems as if Jesus, after reading from the scroll, simply went back to his seat after reading and then added his challenge, almost like an afterthought. It must be remembered that at this time it was traditional to stand to read and to sit to teach. So the description of him standing to read the passage and then sitting down before he spoke fits the customs of his day. Jesus' teaching on that day was very challenging to his hearers. He not only proclaimed himself as the Messiah (anointed one) but also suggested that the Gentiles would be more responsive to his ministry than people from his own home town. His rejection by the people of Nazareth inevitably followed, and from here he moved to Capernaum.

Although this does not exactly describe an average Sabbath in Nazareth, from this passage we can conclude that, before he began his ministry, Jesus was not only a respected member of his synagogue but he was also a regular lay preacher.

Did Jesus break the Sabbath?

In the first century there was continuing discussion about what was and was not permitted on the Sabbath. There were differences of opinion between the Sadducees and the Pharisees, where the Pharisees were more willing to find ways around Sabbath laws but the Sadducees were more literal.[3] Among the Pharisees, there were sometimes heated debates between the more lenient House of Hillel and the stricter House of Shammai. Other groups, such as the Essenes, had an even stricter understanding of the law. All these groups had different interpretations of the basic commands that a person should not work, start a fire or begin a journey.

In Luke 6:1–11 there are two stories where Jesus, or his

disciples, are accused of breaking the Sabbath. In the first, his disciples picked some corn and ate on the Sabbath, and in the second Jesus healed a man with a withered hand. Both of these incidents led to debate over the precise regulations of the Sabbath, but neither would have been seen as severe transgressions of the Sabbath by the vast majority of Jews at that time. Mark adds the important saying of Jesus, 'The Sabbath was made for people, not people for the Sabbath' (Mark 2:27). The Sabbath was given to provide a day of rest in which to honour God. Adding on too many regulations can destroy the joy of the day. David Flusser cites a similar quote from a scribal source, and concludes that Jesus' attitude to the Sabbath was well within the acceptable limits of his day. Like many of the more moderate Jewish teachers, he wanted to guard against excessive regulations and to encourage his followers to find the Sabbath a delight.[4]

From Sabbath to Lord's Day

As a child growing up in a Christian home, I assumed that Sunday was the Sabbath day. As far as I was concerned, the Old Testament command to 'remember the Sabbath day by keeping it holy' (Exodus 20:8) referred to Sunday and instructed that we should not work on that day. It was only when I became exposed to Judaism that I discovered an alternative day for the Sabbath – the original Saturday. Like many Christians who have followed this path, it led to some confusion and the inevitable question, which day really is the Sabbath? To begin to answer this question we need to examine the development of Sunday as a special day in Christianity.

The first Christians, like Jesus, were accustomed to go to synagogue on Saturday and to treat this as their day of rest. Jesus rose on the first day of the week and the belief in the resurrection became central to the faith of these new believers. There is very little New Testament evidence for them meeting on that day in particular, though it is commonly believed that they may have met on Saturday evening (the Jewish start of the first day of the week). The only New Testament description of a Christian meeting on the first day is found in Acts 20:7–12. It is the story of a Christian gathering to celebrate communion together and hear a sermon from Paul, who was leaving the next day. The scene is an evening one: lamps have been lit and Paul spoke until late into the night. A young man dropped off to sleep, fell out of the window and was killed. Paul went downstairs, put his arms around the boy, declared him alive and then returned upstairs to 'break bread', eat and preach until daybreak! The traditional Christian view has set this on Sunday evening but a literal Jewish understanding of the evening of the first day would place it on Saturday evening. If this were the case then Paul would have 'broken bread' in the early hours of Sunday morning and left for his journey on that day. The very early morning communion corroborates early Christian practice for Sunday worship though it later became detached from a meal. It does not indicate that Sunday had been designated as the Sabbath day, however – had this been the case Paul would not have started out on a journey. There are many references to Paul attending synagogue on the Sabbath (Saturday) in Acts and it seems likely that this remained his day of rest. In 1 Corinthians 16:2, Paul encourages the church to set aside a sum of money for alms on the first day of each week. Again this becomes the pattern in the early church, who took a collection for the poor each Sunday, but it does not tally with the hypothesis that Sunday had become the Sabbath, since handling money is an act of work.

The apostle John described himself as being in the Spirit on the 'Lord's Day' (Revelation 1:10). Though there is no indication that he meant Sunday, this title had become fixed to the first day of the week by early in the second century AD. The term retained the strong end-times connotations of the

Hebrew Bible (Isaiah 13:6) and it was seen not so much as the first day but as the eighth day. This was thought to be symbolic of the ultimate paradise beyond the tribulations of this age, and each Sunday would be a foretaste of heaven, as Communion was a foretaste of the messianic banquet to come. This is not unlike a Jewish concept that Sabbath was a glimpse of the Eden we have lost, and was probably a development of the teaching on a final Sabbath rest in Hebrews 4.

Sunday became the regular day of worship for Christians in the very early years of the church, but it did not become established as a day of rest – a Christian Sabbath – until much later. In 321 AD, Constantine declared Sunday to be a day free from work. This may have been from a Christian motivation, though there are strong indications that Constantine retained much of his previous sun worship and Sunday was the sun's day. After the Roman Empire, other rulers in Europe periodically sought to maintain Sunday as a 'holiday' and ensure that Christians attended church. Strict keeping of Sunday as a Sabbath only finally arose out of the Scottish and English Reformation.

In the Jewish community the change from Saturday to Sunday as a day for corporate worship was seen as an anti-Jewish statement. Indeed, the Council of Laodicea in AD 364 ordained that Sunday should be the day for Christian worship and Christians should work on Saturday rather than 'Judaise'. Though the reasons for changing the day were considerably more complex than simply an anti-Jewish reaction by Gentile Christians, it continues to provide a divide between the two religions. Until recent years, a Jewish person who became a follower of Jesus would have to worship on Sunday rather than Saturday to be part of their new faith community. Today, the considerable growth of Messianic Jewish congregations in Israel and elsewhere enables Jewish followers of Jesus to have their regular worship on Saturdays and retain a Jewish approach to the rhythm of the week.

Sabbath in later Judaism

The meaning of the Sabbath

The themes of Creation, Covenant and Rest underlie the Jewish understanding of Sabbath. God created Shabbat to give time for his whole creation to rest and he commanded his covenant people to observe the Sabbath as a sign that they were his people and that he was their God. It is a step back into Eden when we can temporarily enjoy life without toil. It is above all a family time when relatives come together to worship and rest. In the Middle Ages a tradition developed to see the Sabbath as a bride for Israel who would come each Friday night, making the Sabbath a kind of weekly wedding celebration.

Friday night

Friday is very much a part of the Sabbath traditions. In observant Orthodox homes the women will spend the morning preparing for Shabbat, making sure there is enough food for the day. These will be the most special meals of the week, perhaps gefilte fish for Friday evening and cholent for Saturday lunch. I have heard that slow cookers were invented by Orthodox Jews. Challah bread and wine must be bought, together with any fresh foods. Sometimes the men buy these on the way home from work together with the traditional bunch of flowers for their wives. If you go to Jerusalem, it is an experience to visit Mahane Yehuda Market on Friday afternoons. You will find it heaving with people looking as if they are shopping for a siege, and the traditional Sabbath foods will be very much in evidence.

Just before the Sabbath comes in, it is traditional for the woman of the house to light Sabbath candles, which are placed on the dining table. Usually two candles will be lit, though in some homes an extra candle is lit for each child. Depending on the time of year, this will frequently happen well before the meal is eaten. It is the last work to be performed and should never happen after Shabbat has begun. For this reason the woman screens her eyes from the flame with her hand before she says the traditional blessing, 'Blessed are you O Lord our God, King of the Universe, who has sanctified us by your commandments and commanded us to light the Sabbath lights.' Once the blessing has been said, she removes her hand, says the traditional greeting 'Shabbat Shalom' (Sabbath peace) and the Sabbath has begun.

While the women are home, the men go to synagogue to welcome in the Sabbath. This is literally done through a beautiful ceremony known as Kabbalat Shabbat. The door of the synagogue is opened and the congregation turns towards it. The Sabbath is welcomed as a bride, 'Come my friend and meet the bride, let us welcome the presence of the Sabbath.' This is based on a very ancient tradition, but became popular through the kabbalists of Safed in Galilee.

Once home, the traditional Shabbat meal can begin. Blessings are said over the wine, 'Blessed are you O Lord our God, King of the Universe, who gives us the fruit of the vine'; and then the Shabbat bread, 'Blessed are you O Lord our God, King of the Universe, who brings forth bread from the earth.' Each is passed around in turn and the bread is eaten dipped in salt. After this there are Sabbath songs, and the father will bless each of his children in turn. It is traditional for him to read the portion from Proverbs 31 to his wife, 'A wife of noble character who can find? She is worth more than rubies. Her husband has full confidence in her and lacks nothing of value.' After this there are further prayers and Sabbath songs. Once the ceremonial part is complete the meal can begin.

Saturday

My first ever visit to an Orthodox synagogue for Shabbat was to one of the oldest and most famous synagogues in central London. We telephoned a few days before to make sure they would welcome non-Jewish visitors and to find the service times. We were told the service began at 8.00 am and so we duly turned up just a little beforehand. The synagogue was very empty at the beginning and it soon became apparent that very few people went to the whole service, which lasted about three hours, and most people arrived a little later. As a woman I was able to sit upstairs in a gallery and could look down on the men who led the service. The singing was beautiful. At one point everyone stood and sang the Shema: 'Hear O Israel, the Lord our God, the Lord is one. Blessed be his name whose glorious kingdom is for ever and ever' (Deuteronomy 6:4).

This is the central commandment in Judaism and was a popular summary of the law at the time of Jesus. The service continued, and soon the doors of the Ark – a cupboard at the front of the synagogue – were opened. Inside were a number of Torah scrolls, wrapped in beautifully embroidered covers with special ornaments on the spindles. One scroll was removed from the Ark and processed through the synagogue to the Bimah or reading desk at the centre. The scroll was opened and the portion for the week was read. When the scroll had been read (it was several chapters), it was returned to the Ark and the service gradually came towards a conclusion. Once the service had ended, we were invited to join the congregation in another room for Kiddush. We were given a glass of sweet Shabbat wine and offered a selection of small cakes.

This was an Orthodox synagogue, so the women were separate and the entire service was conducted in Hebrew. Reform and Liberal synagogues are more modern and families will sit together for the service. Some of the service will be in English and there will usually be a sermon.

The Shabbat lift

As society has progressed, the rabbis have had to find new interpretations of the basic Sabbath commands to keep Sabbath as a day of rest. The story below from our kibbutz weekend well illustrates this theme.

It was a mile back to our kibbutz hotel from the shady (and unobservant) station café where we had sipped an Israeli 'Maccabee' beer, waiting for the midday heat to subside a little. In the early afternoon the uphill walk was still a considerable challenge (we later discovered that this was the hottest May weekend since 1942). The hotel eventually towered above us. We risked a short cut, scrambling up a rough path and thankfully finding some steps leading towards the hotel. As I staggered into the lobby, I knew that I must be a darker shade of beetroot. Our room was only one floor up but the lift seemed very inviting. We entered and pushed for our floor. To our surprise we went down a floor, waited an age and then the doors closed again. We pushed for our floor but still the lift went down, stopping at each floor for at least a minute. Then the truth dawned: this was a Shabbat lift! Throughout the day it would run, stopping at each floor and giving plenty of time for the people to get in. Our room receded above us. It was a choice of a long wait or an awful lot of stairs.

The Shabbat lift symbolises the modern problems with observing Shabbat. The rabbis have decided that it is permissible to *continue* to use any electrical appliance, but not to push a button or turn a switch to *start* one – that would be work because it would 'start a flame'. So lights, heating and ovens can only be used if they are left on all the time or used with a timer switch, hence the Shabbat lift. Our kibbutz hotel was not so large – imagine living in an apartment block on the nineteenth floor.

The end of Shabbat

One of the most moving places to watch the end of Shabbat is at the Western Wall in Jerusalem. As the Sabbath ends, long rows of young men linked arm in arm descend on the Western Wall. They are familiar with the traditional Israeli dance steps and sing Sabbath songs with beautiful harmonies.

Up in the hills in the kibbutz hotel, an Orthodox Bar

Mitzvah group was having a special party in a function room. Older couples drifted around in the evening sun and children played. As the sun went down, a group of Orthodox men started chanting from their prayer books on the hotel terrace – all facing Jerusalem. Below in the lobby a large American explained to his children that they had to wait until two stars could be seen before Shabbat could end.

The stars came out and the dressed up 'Shabbatness' melted away. Soon families began to leave, crossing the hotel lawns in the gathering dark. Now they were in shorts, carrying their Shabbat clothes on hangers. There was a flurry of cars starting and even the 'Egged' bus arrived. Within an hour the hotel seemed deserted and only the tourists were left.

Havdalah is a special ceremony to end Shabbat. The word means 'separation' and it marks the separation between the sacred and the secular. We leave Eden behind for another week and look toward six days of work. Havdalah involves all the senses: a special cup is filled to overflowing, symbolising the abundant blessings of God; a candle made of many wicks is lit and burns fiercely (this can only be extinguished in the wine which has spilled out of the glass into a saucer beneath it); and finally a special spice box is passed around. Song of Songs ends with a reference to spices as the lovers part (8:14). Sabbath is seen as the bride of Israel and, as the sweet spices are passed around, we remember the fragrance of our bride through the coming week.[5] Thus all the senses are involved as we bid goodbye to the Sabbath and the family is ready to start the week.

Making the link

One of the questions we began with was should Christians celebrate Sabbath on Saturday or Sunday? We have seen that the development of Sunday happened early in the church but that it only gradually became a Sabbath. My personal view is that it is more important to apply the teaching of Sabbath regularly to one day a week than to one particular day of the week. In Israel, Saturday is the regular day off in the week and most Messianic congregations and also many international congregations choose to meet on this day. In other parts of the world, most Christians meet for worship on Sundays. Some Christians with many responsibilities in church do find that a Saturday Sabbath for rest and family time can be quite liberating, and frees them to give their energies wholeheartedly to Sunday as the day to 'work' to provide worship for others. In this case some of the themes of Sabbath become spread over both days and produce a pattern that may even have similarities with the early church.

In our very busy society it is important for us to regain the teaching of Sabbath and make the time to take a day of rest. If we do so, we will indeed come to find the Sabbath a delight.

Your own family Sabbath

The tradition of welcoming in the Sabbath on Friday evenings has become an important one in our home. At the end of a busy week, even if we are taking our Sabbath on Sunday not Saturday, we keep Friday evenings as a special time to unwind, relax and to pray together.

Family prayers for the Sabbath

We have gradually developed an order of service for Fridays which is based very loosely on the Friday night meal experienced in Jewish homes. It is adapted for believers in Jesus and does not pretend to be a genuine Jewish Sabbath order. I aimed to combine the principle of a fellowship meal together with a time for prayers with and for family and friends. Some of the prayers are adapted from the Jewish prayer book, some are taken from the Bible. You will find this liturgy at the end of the chapter.

You will need:
Candles: Traditionally two candles are lit by the mother of the household. As this is an adaptation, please feel free to be creative about this. It would be in the spirit of the meal to have an additional one for each child present.

Wine: Wine is an important part of the Sabbath meal. If it is not normal in your home, grape juice is quite permissible. You might like to find one special cup or glass to pass around, or it is also acceptable for each person to have a glass.

Bread: The traditional bread is a plaited 'challah' loaf but any bread would do. You should have two loaves on the table, but these can be two rolls if there are very few of you. If possible find plaited bread. (It is not unknown for my husband to say 'On the table are two . . .' and then lift the challah cover to discover if there is anything resembling Sabbath bread. Sometimes all he discovers are a couple of pieces of brown sliced!)

Salt: This is the third significant food which makes up the ceremonial part of the meal. It is sprinkled on a piece of bread before being eaten.

The meal

The Sabbath prayers are said before the meal is eaten. It is therefore important to have something cooking that can stay warm while this is taking place. In a Jewish home, the Friday night meal would be the best meal of the week and the family might well 'dress up' a bit for it.

Further ideas

You may like to include songs amongst the prayers. This would happen in an Orthodox home. As you use this order you may find you make changes to suit your own particular family or group of friends.

Making a cover for Challah bread

Challah bread is traditionally covered at the start of a meal. Some people say this is to represent the dew that covered the manna in the wilderness, whereas others say it is to prevent the bread noticing that the wine has a blessing first! Either way, it is a good principle to cover food before it is used.

You will need:

A piece of cross-stitch fabric, roughly 12 in by 18 in (30 cm by 45 cm)

Embroidery threads of different colours
Cotton thread of the same colour as your fabric.

My cover has a design based on the Menorah in the Temple. You may like to make your own design, which might be a creation theme, wheat, or another symbol such as a Star of David. The colour of the fabric and the thread can be varied according to your own home colours.

Cut your fabric to the required size, making sure that you have removed any selvage edge. Iron to make sure you have a completely flat surface. Next, using a sewing machine with the cotton thread, sew a zigzag line ¾ in (2 cm) in from the edge, right around the fabric. This should ideally be the one square width all the way around. If you do not have a sewing machine, make this edge by hand using cross-stitch. Now you can make a fringe around the fabric by removing the threads which lie outside the border. Next make the border using the holes in the fabric for cross-stitch. Be careful not to pull the stitches too tightly and iron the cloth once it has been completed. Now you are ready to stitch your design, again using cross-stitch. You may like to mark it in pencil before you start to stitch. Be very careful not to pull the stitches (an embroidery hoop may help keep the design flat). Finally iron your cover again and it will be ready to use.

Youth track

Try to find out about the advantages of a Sabbath rest. You could visit your local library or, if you have access to the World Wide Web, you might like to use a web browser. Can you find any information concerning the physical benefits of a day off each week? What are the laws in different countries and do other religions take days other than Saturday or Sunday?

Recipes

Challah bread

Challah is made from a rich dough with egg and sometimes some added sugar. On Sabbath eve a family will have two plaited loaves of challah on the table. For Shavuot and other festivals it is more traditional to have round loaves.

For 2 loaves

1 packet (⅓ oz / 7g) easy blend yeast
9 fl oz (250 ml) warm water
4 oz (110 g) sugar
1½ lbs (700 g) plain white flour
4 oz (110 g) oil
2 large eggs, beaten
1 teaspoon salt
1 egg to glaze
poppy or sesame seeds

Sift 1lb of the flour and the salt into a large mixing bowl and mix in the dry yeast. Dissolve the sugar in the water. Add to the flour and yeast, mixing thoroughly. Add the oil and then the eggs mixing both into the dough. Add the remaining flour and knead until the dough is soft and elastic. Place the dough into a greased bowl and turn so that all sides are greased. Cover with a towel and put aside for about two hours for the dough to double in size (dough will rise at room temperature and this gives a better result). Punch down and knead a few times.

To make a plaited loaf

Divide the dough in half for two large loaves (when there are just two of us, I prefer to divide this amount of dough into six and have six much smaller loaves, four of which I freeze for later weeks). Each piece will be made into a separate loaf. Take one piece and divide into four. Set one of these smaller pieces aside and roll out each of the other three between your hands to make thick ropes. Lay these out onto a floured surface. Join them at one end and make them into a loose plait. Divide the fourth piece into three parts and make a smaller plait in a similar way. Place this plait on top of the larger one, gently pushing it down at either end. Cover the loaves loosely and let them rise at room temperature again for about half an hour. Brush with the egg glaze and then sprinkle with poppy seeds. Bake at 200°C (400°F, gas mark 6) for 40 to 45 minutes.

To make a round loaf for festivals

Take half the dough and divide it into two pieces – one piece should be approximately twice the size of the other. Smooth both into ball shapes, then put the larger piece down onto a board and flatten a little. Take the smaller piece, place this on top and flatten so that it pushes slightly into the other loaf. Push a dent into the very top using your finger so that it resembles a cottage loaf. Cover the loaves loosely and let them rise at room temperature again for about half an hour. Brush with the egg glaze and then sprinkle with seeds (hundreds and thousands are sometimes used for Shavuot). Bake at 200°C (400°F, gas mark 6) for 40 to 45 minutes.

For children

Give them a small piece of dough to make their own Sabbath loaf. They might like to try plaiting it or making it into some other shape. Extra ingredients such as chocolate drops may be added, and have plenty of hundreds and thousands to cover the surface.

Gefilte fish

For 4 people

8 oz (230 g) boned, white fish
1 onion

1 grated carrot
1 large egg
1 tablespoon oil
1 tablespoon cold water
2–3 tablespoons matzah meal (or bread crumbs)
3 tablespoons finely chopped parsley or dill
A little grated lemon rind
Salt and pepper to taste

Put the onion and fish in a food processor and mince together. Add the egg, oil, matzah meal, parsley and lemon rind. Add the carrot and mix until well combined. Form the ingredients into small balls by rolling them in your hands. Steam cook the fish balls in a greased steamer for 15 minutes.

I sometimes make a less traditional tuna gefilte fish loaf. In this case use one tin of tuna in oil rather than the white fish and omit the oil and water in preparation. Spoon the mixture into a small greased loaf tin and cover with foil. Bake in a moderate oven (180°C, 350°F, gas mark 4) for about 45 minutes. Gefilte fish is great served with a relish made out of horseradish, mayonnaise and puréed cooked beetroot.

Cholent for Sabbath lunch

This is a marvellous recipe if you are tied up with services in the morning and still want to entertain at lunchtime!

For 6 people

12 oz (340 g) stewing steak
3 oz (85 g) haricot or butter beans
2 oz (55 g) pearl barley
1 onion, chopped
2 garlic cloves (optional)
2 carrots, thickly sliced
3 potatoes, thickly sliced

A bay leaf
1 teaspoon paprika
1 teaspoon ginger
1 tablespoon cooking oil
Salt and pepper to season
A stock cube if desired
½ pt boiling water

You will need a slow cooker, or a casserole dish with a tight fitting lid and a very low setting on your oven. This dish begins cooking the day before it is needed.

First, pre-soak beans for 12 hours in cold water or 4 hours in boiling water (follow instructions on packet, if given). Boil hard in unsalted water for at least ten minutes before adding to the slow cooker which should be brought up to heat. In a large pan, sauté the onions and meat in oil with the spices. Add the water, potato and carrot. Heat through and then transfer all the ingredients to the slow cooker. Cook for one hour on high and then turn to low and leave overnight. Do not look at the dish for at least 12 hours. It can then be served at any time.

Sabbath Prayers for Believers in Jesus

The Sabbath starts with the lighting of candles by the woman of the house. Before the candles are lit the following is said:

Lord of the universe, I am about to kindle lights in honour of the Sabbath, even as it is written: 'and you shall call the Sabbath a delight, and the holy day of the Lord honourable'. May streams of living water flow upon me and upon mine, may you be gracious to us and may your presence dwell with us.

Father of Mercy, continue your loving kindness to me and my dear ones. May my family walk in the way of righteousness before you, loyal to your word and holding to good deeds. Keep far from us all manner of shame, grief and care; and grant that peace, light and joy ever abide in our home. For with you is the fountain of life, and in your light do we see light. Amen.[6]

Candles are lit and the following blessings said by the woman of the household:

(Baruch ata Adonai Eloheinu melech ha olam. Asher kidishanu b'ruach ha kodesh, v natan lanu et Yeshua ha Mashiah l'hiot ora ha olam.)

Blessed are you, O Lord our God, King of the Universe, who has sanctified us by your Holy Spirit and given us Jesus to be the light of the world.

Everyone says the following from Psalm 95:

O come let us worship the Lord; let us shout for joy before the rock of our salvation.
Let us come before him with thanksgiving and extol him with music and song.
For the Lord is a great God and a great king above all gods.
In his hand are the deep places of the earth, and the mountain peaks belong to him.

SABBATH – REST AND PRAYER WITH THE FAMILY **197**

The sea is his for he made it, and his hands formed the dry land.
O come let us worship and bow down; let us kneel before the Lord our maker.
For he is our God, and we are the people of his pasture; and the flock under his care.

The father of the house reads the following:

The heavens and the earth were completed in their vast array, and God saw all that he had made and it was very good. God had finished the work he had been doing, so on the seventh day he rested from all his work. And God blessed the seventh day and made it holy, because he rested from all the work of creating that he had done.

A reminder of God's blessings on us

The father of the house now pours a cup of wine. Wine is a symbol of joy in the Hebrew scriptures and of the abundant blessing which God gives us.
The father says the following blessing:

(Baruch ata Adonai, Eloheinu melech ha olam, borai p'ree hagafen.)

Blessed are you, O Lord our God, King of the Universe, who creates the fruit of the vine. Blessed are you for giving us Jesus to be the true Vine.

All drink some wine.

A reminder of God's provision for us

On the table are two Sabbath loaves. These remind us of God's provision in the wilderness. On the first five days of the week he provided enough manna for that day but on the sixth day he gave a double provision so there was no need to work on the

Sabbath. We are reminded of God's many provisions for our needs.

The father lifts the bread and says the following blessing:

(Baruch ata Adonai, Eloheinu melech ha olam, ha motzi lechem min ha aretz.)

Blessed are you, O Lord our God, King of the Universe, who brings forth bread from the earth.

A piece of bread is broken off by each person, sprinkled with salt, and then eaten.

Another person may say the following:

Rejoice in the Lord always, I will say it again: Rejoice! Let your gentleness be evident to all. The Lord is near. Do not be anxious about anything, but by prayer and petition, with thanksgiving, present your requests to God. And the peace of God which transcends all understanding will guard your hearts and your minds in Messiah Jesus. (Philippians 4:4–7)

If there are children in the home the following may be said by all:

Then children were brought to Jesus for him to place his hands on them and pray for them ... Jesus said, 'Let the little children come to me, for the kingdom of heaven belongs to all who come to me like children.' Then he placed his hands on them and blessed them. (Matthew 19:13–14)

Prayers may be said for children.

The men may wish to say the traditional Sabbath blessing from Proverbs 31 (page 184) and then pray for their wives, in which case the women alone should say the next part and then pray for their husbands.

All say the following from the words of Song of Songs 8:7:

Many waters cannot quench love; rivers cannot wash it away. If one were to give all the wealth of his house for love, it would be utterly scorned.

Prayers may be said for close loved ones.

Another person may say the following:

Be devoted to one another in brotherly love. Honour one another above yourselves. Never lose enthusiasm to serve the Lord. Be joyful in hope, patient in affliction, faithful in prayer. Share with God's people who are in need. Rejoice with those who rejoice; mourn with those who mourn. Live in harmony with one another. (Romans 12:10–16, abbrev.)

Prayers may be said for wider friends and family.

Let us end our Sabbath prayers with the following blessing from Numbers 6:24–26:
The Lord bless us and keep us,
The Lord make his face to shine upon us and be gracious to us,
The Lord lift up his countenance towards us and give us his peace.

The meal is now served.

Notes

1. Glinert, L., *The Joys of Hebrew* (Oxford University Press: New York, 1992), p. 202.
2. Sacks, J., *Faith in the Future* (Darton, Longman and Todd: London, 1995), p.134.
3. Sanders, E. P., *Jewish Law from Jesus to the Mishnah* (SCM Press: London, and Trinity Press International: Philadelphia, 1990), pp. 8–9.

4. Flusser, D., *Jesus* (The Magnes Press: The Hebrew University, Jerusalem, 1998), p. 62.
5. Neot Kedumim, *The Biblical Landscape Reserve in Israel*, Trail A (Neot Kedumim: Israel,1992), pp. 27–33.
6. Some of these prayers are loosely based on Simeon Singer's daily prayer book.

Chapter Eleven

AS THE SEASONS CLOSE

'How long have you known Yeshua?' It was Friday night and I was visiting a Messianic fellowship in North London. I had moved to Finchley a few months before, having just graduated from All Nations – a cross cultural and international Bible college that mainly equips Christians to work overseas. I had been a Christian for over twenty years but at that moment I felt as if I hardly knew 'Yeshua', this very Jewish Jesus I was just beginning to encounter. It was not that I had come with a caricatured image of a Gentile Jesus with blond hair and blue eyes. I had always known that Jesus was Jewish, but, before, he had always come to *me*, spoken my language and understood my life. In those first few months in London, I felt as if Jesus (or Yeshua as everyone called him[1]) had invited me over to his culture and I suddenly found him completely at home in a totally different context. I thought of my fellow students from All Nations, scattered all over the world and working in far more challenging conditions. As they grappled with different cultures and religions, it was possible to go back to the Bible and relate to a Jesus familiar to them. For me, when I turned to the scriptures, I found instead that Jesus really was Yeshua and fitted the culture I had joined far more than the one I had left very far behind. I was in culture shock and it was probing into the very core of my faith.

Thankfully that uncomfortable feeling was a transitory one. It did return at different times, but, as I became at home with the culture, so things began to integrate together. I joined a small group of Jewish believers in Jesus, or Messianic Jews, that met each Saturday to read the Torah portion for the week and share the day together. Gradually, I became comfortable with the culture and 'learnt the language' of Judaism (literally, to some extent – there are many Hebrew classes in that area). As I became familiar with Jesus as Yeshua, I began to come to know him in a far deeper way than I had ever done before. My work with CMJ gave me the excuse to make fairly regular trips to Israel, where I also met up with local believers in Jesus, both Jewish and Arab. As I came to know the land of the Bible, the climate, the culture, and most importantly the people, so the Bible took on a totally different dimension – as did my faith.

Now the opposite began to happen. In my church one Sunday a sermon was preached on a Gospel reading. It was an incredibly Jewish passage but this was not mentioned. I felt like jumping up and down on my seat, and was only thankful that my vicar was an encouraging and understanding person. More recently, I went to a concert of Bach's St John's Passion. We had been to St Matthew's Passion the year before and I was really looking forward to it, but this was John's Gospel, which is not always complimentary about 'the Jews' and this time it was sung in German. As the mentions of 'Juden' became more frequent and more negative, I found my heart beating faster and prickles on the back of my neck. Emotionally, I felt very Jewish and very threatened.

Understanding Jesus

Through understanding Jesus in his Jewish family context, I have come to a fuller understanding of the Christian faith. A key part of this for me has been the festivals. Judaism is as much something you do as something you believe and, as I have lived through the festival year, so I have understood better the rhythm of life that Jesus also experienced. His childhood family holidays were spent in Jerusalem at Passover each year. Maybe he went with his father and brothers on a second visit in the autumn to celebrate Sukkot. He knew a Sabbath that went from Friday night to Saturday night. He travelled the land of Israel, knew the trees and their tithing laws, made huppahs from their wood, and knew a myriad of other small things about Israel and the Jewish world that I had also come to know and love.

I have also had to disentangle the things that would have certainly not been a part of Jesus' world. In Messianic circles, it sometimes seems as if Jesus could quite easily be found sitting in a kosher deli, wearing a kippah and saying 'Oy vey already', while tucking into a plate of gefilte fish. Yes, Jesus would have kept kosher and would probably have covered his head, but kippahs are post biblical, and the rest is Eastern European culture. This does not make it necessarily a problem, for example, to present Jesus this way in a drama, but it is similar to portraying him in jeans and a tee shirt to relate to Western youth culture. Jewish culture has not been frozen in time since the New Testament, but Jesus can relate to all generations and cultures, Jewish and Gentile.

A choice between festivals?

The question this poses is should Christians leave behind the traditional culture of Western Christianity and move more towards biblical Judaism? In particular, should we change from Christian festivals to Jewish ones? For many Christians, this hangs on the question 'are Jewish festivals more biblical?' and this needs to be addressed first.

There is no doubt that Passover, Pentecost and the High Holy Days were the festivals of the Old and New Testaments.

Christmas and Easter were unknown to anyone who features in the Bible. However, the Christmas and Easter stories are part of the Gospel accounts, and the death and resurrection of Jesus are at the core of Christian faith. 'Easter' as a name has roots in a pagan spring festival, but many European languages have a name for this festival that derives from Passover. It would be strange for a Christian to remember the Last Supper in Passover without going on to remember both the death of Jesus and his resurrection. Biblical historians believe that there were pre-biblical precursors to Passover. Israel may have taken a festival that was already being celebrated and transformed it into one that was centred on God and his salvation of them through the Exodus.

Christmas as a date has pagan roots and coincides with the winter solstice, which sun worshippers saw as the rebirth of their god. There are many traditions that go back to pre-Christian origins, such as bringing holly and ivy into the house, or secular origins such as having a Christmas tree. The story of Christmas is highly biblical, however, and arguably more so than Hanukkah. This simply celebrates the rededication of the Temple on the anniversary of its desecration, which was itself on a pagan holiday.

If the Jewish festival cycle is biblical in contrast to the Christian festival cycle, which was unknown to Jesus, individual festivals from each calendar have biblical origins and outside influences. As Jewish and Christian festivals have developed, they have transformed traditions of older festivals by focussing the celebration on God and his actions for us. So which should we celebrate?

A way forward

A key thing to remember is that festivals are about community. Although they can be celebrated in isolation and this has happened to both Jews and Christians in different times, this is not the norm and, providing they are God-centred, it is most important to celebrate the feasts of your own faith community. For Jewish believers in Jesus this may mean continuing to follow the Jewish festival path. In doing so there will be all the richness of being in rhythm with the biblical year and the practicality of being in tune with the culture outside. This would be especially true in Israel or areas where there is a very high population of Jewish people. The challenge in this instance is to keep alive the transformation that Yeshua brings to the festival year when this is not known in the surrounding culture. Not every Jewish believer would wish to take this path. Some, particularly in a predominately Gentile Christian context, are quite happy in a mainstream church and following the Christian year. They may call themselves Hebrew Christians, or simply Christians! That is their choice and it must be respected. For others it is more of a halfway house, mainly worshipping in church but seeking to come together on an occasional basis with other Jewish Christians. Here, festival gatherings become particularly important and an enhancement to faith.

Very much the same advice can be given to Gentile Christians. If you are a Christian but have never experienced the Jewish festivals, I would strongly encourage you to do so at least once for the biblical understanding they will bring. Some Gentile Christians are called by God to join the Jewish followers of Jesus in a very integral way. Again this will usually be in Israel or very Jewish areas, and for some it means leaving behind the culture of their Gentile Christian faith. This is an unusual situation. Most Christians who are interested in Jewish roots to the Christian faith find that their role is actually to be a bridge between the two cultures, enjoying the fullness of the Jewish festivals, whilst also celebrating the Christian ones with their church.

A double feast

My experience of Jewish festivals has caused me to look more thoughtfully at Christian ones. After six years in Jewish North London, I married and moved to Oxford. The church I joined celebrated the traditional festivals and I suddenly discovered a topography to the church year that I had not understood before. I found that many of the festivals of the Christian year had themes in common with those of the Jewish calendar. Thus, Advent has similarities with Rosh Hashanah as we look towards God coming among us, first as Messiah, and one day as King to judge the living and the dead. Christmas continues the theme of God's presence with us and together with Epiphany, links to the Feast of Tabernacles when, after the Second Coming of Jesus, all the nations will come to worship the living God. Lent has similarities with Yom Kippur, with our need for self-examination and repentance. Easter very clearly links to Passover and the major theme of redemption. Finally, Christian and Jewish Pentecost have the combined themes of first fruits, harvest and God making his covenant with his people. This is a special time to remember the Holy Spirit, Shekinah of the Lord, who now dwells among us.

The purpose of a festival cycle is to regularly remember God's action in history, so that we grasp these concepts of repentance, redemption, salvation and atonement that might otherwise be beyond us. The outcome of a strong, faith-centred festival year should be that we become bound together as a community, so that together we come closer to God and experience his presence among us.

In our home we have a double feast. On Friday nights we celebrate Shabbat and use the time for family prayers. On Sunday we are in church, meeting for worship with other local Christians. Our actual day off depends on our work schedules and may not be either day. In the autumn, we supplement the Christian ideas of harvest with the biblical teaching of Sukkot.

As Christmas approaches, we light both an Advent candle and our Hanukkah lights to remind us that Jesus continues to come to us as a light to the world and a servant among us. Passover and Easter are again combined, and Pentecost means so much more when you can visualise the events at the Temple on that first post-resurrection Shavuot.

This has become our way. Now I invite you to find yours as you enjoy the Feast of Seasons that God has laid out for us.

Note

1. 'Jesus' is the anglicised form of the Greek translation of the name, 'Yeshua', which is Christ's original name in Hebrew. It is pronounced *Y-shoo-a*.

BIBLIOGRAPHY

Black, N., *Celebration, The Book of Jewish festivals* (Collins: London, 1987)

Booker, R., *Jesus in the feasts of Israel* (Destiny Image Publishers: Shippensburg, Pennsylvania, 1987)

Bradshaw, P., *Early Christian Worship* (SPCK: London, 1996)

Bruce, F. F., 'The book of the Acts', *The New International Commentary on the New Testament* (Wm. B. Eerdmans Publishing Company: Grand Rapids, Michigan, 1990)

Chadwick, H., *The Early Church* (Penguin: London, 1967.)

Encyclopaedia Judaica CD ROM Edition, Version 1.0. (Judaica Multimedia (Israel) Ltd; text: Keter Publishing house Ltd: Jerusalem, 1997)

Edersheim, A., *Jesus the Messiah* (Longman, Green and Company: London, 1889)

Edersheim, A., *The Temple* (The Religious Tract Society: London, c.1880; reprinted: Wm. B. Eerdmans Publishing Company: Grand Rapids, Michigan, 1979)

Epstein, I., (ed.), *The Soncino Talmud* (The Soncino Press: London, 1935–1952)

Flusser, D., *Judaism and the Origins of Christianity* (The Magnes Press: The Hebrew University, Jerusalem, 1988.)

Flusser, D., *Jesus* (The Magnes Press: The Hebrew University, Jerusalem, 1998)

Glinert, L., *The Joys of Hebrew* (Oxford University Press: New York, 1992)

Goodman, P., *The Shavuot Anthology* (The Jewish Publication Society of America: New York, 1974)

Hareuveni, N., *Nature in Our Biblical Heritage* (Neot Kedumim: Israel, 1980)

Hodson, M. R., *Jerusalem's Story* (Olive Press: St Albans, 1998.)

Hodson, M. R., *Pentecost Beginnings, a Resource Pack for Churches and Groups* (Olive Press: St Albans, 1998)

Hughes, P. E., *A Commentary on the Epistle to the Hebrews* (Wm. B. Eerdmans Publishing Company: Grand Rapids, Michigan, 1977)

Johnstone, P., *Operation World* (STL/WEC: Bromley, 1993 (fifth edition)

Neot Kedumim, *The Biblical Landscape Reserve in Israel*, Trail A. (Neot Kedumim: Israel, 1992)

Notley, S., 'Discovering the Jerusalem of Jesus', *Bible Times*, vol. 1, no. 1 (1988)

Raphael, C., *The Festivals, A history of Jewish Celebration* (George Weidenfeld & Nicholson Ltd: London, 1990)

Renburg, D. F., *The Complete Family Guide to Jewish holidays* (Robson Books: London, 1987)

Riggans, W., *In Every Generation, a Seder For Believers in Yeshua* (All Nations Christian College: Ware, 1987)

Rose, A., (ed), *Judaism and Ecology* (Cassell Publishers Ltd: London, 1992)

Roth, C., (ed), *Encyclopaedia Judaica* (Keter Publishing House Ltd: Jerusalem, 1972)

Runes, D., (ed), *Dictionary of Judaism* (Citadel Press: Secaucus, New Jersey, 1959)

Sacks, J., *Faith in the Future* (Darton, Longman and Todd: London, 1995)

Safrai, C., 'Jesus' Jewish Parents', *Jerusalem Perspective*, vol. 40 (Sept/Oct 1993), pp.10–11, 14–15

Sanders, E. P., *Jewish Law from Jesus to the Mishnah* (SCM Press: London, and Trinity Press International: Philadelphia, 1990)

Schauss, H., *The Jewish Festivals* (Jewish Chronicle Publications: London, 1986)

Schernan, N. and Zlotowitz, M., *The Family Haggadah* (Mesorah Publications, Ltd: New York, 1981)

Shanks, H., (ed), *Christianity and Rabbinic Judaism* (SPCK: London, 1993)

Singer, S., *The Authorised Daily Prayer Book of the United Hebrew Congregations of the British Commonwealth of Nations* (Eyre and Spottiswoode Publishers: London, 1962)

Steinsaltz, A., *The Essential Talmud* (Basic Books, Inc: New York, 1976)

Strassfeld, M., *The Jewish holidays, A Guide and Commentary* (Harper and Row: New York, 1985)

Testet, B., (ed), *Harvest Roots, a Resource Pack for Churches and Groups* (Olive Press: St Albans, 1994)

Wilson, M., *Our Father Abraham* (Wm. B. Eerdmans Publishing Company: Grand Rapids, Michigan, 1989)

Uval, B., *Seder Tu b'Shvat* (Neot Kedumim: Israel, 1998)

Young, B., *The Jewish Background to the Lord's Prayer* (Center for Judaic-Christian Studies: Austin, Texas, 1984)

Young, B., *The Parables, Jewish Tradition and Christian Interpretation* (Hendrickson Publishers: Massachusetts, 1998)

INDEX

Advent 128, 146, 206, 207
Afikomen 9, 39, 41, 60, 63–64
Akiva 26
Apocrypha 142, 144
Ark of the Covenant 102, 104, 123
Ashkenazi 9, 25, 57, 98, 107
Atonement 102, 105, 106, 110
Aviv 31

Babylon 11, 23–25, 90, 124
Bar Kockba 9, 23, 26
Bar Mitzvah 9, 75
Bikkurim 10, 26, 68–70
Blood Libel 46
Book of Life 91

Calendar, Jewish 26–28, 206
Crafts:
  Bible, book jacket 113
  Challah bread cover 190
  Fruit of the Spirit tree 81
  Gingerbread tabernacle 135
  Grow your own tree 158
  Hanukkah lights 147
  Matzah cover 52
  New Year cards 96
  Noisemakers 167
  Purim masks 168
Creation 20, 71, 90–91, 95, 151–159, 174–175, 183

Day of Atonement 17, 26, 101–117
Days of Awe 87, 91, 106
Dedication, Feast of 11, 141–150
Diaspora 23, 74, 125, 131

Easter 31, 40, 43–44, 46, 50, 204, 206, 207
Epiphany 206
Essenes 22, 41, 74, 179
Esther, Feast of 14, 161–171
Etrog 10, 121

Fasting 16, 17, 26, 27, 76, 101, 107, 109, 162

First Fruits 10, 26, 39–43, 67–70, 74–77, 80, 206
Four questions 38–39, 46, 60–61
Four species 10, 12, 120–121, 125, 132

Gemara 10, 16, 24
Goodly tree, fruit of the 10, 120

Haftorah 10, 178
Haggadah 10, 45, 51, 59–65
Hagigah 10, 42
Hallel 10, 37, 39, 125–126, 143
Hanukkah 11, 26, 124, 141–150, 204, 207
Hassidic movement 25
Hasmoneans 11, 145
Havdalah 11, 187
Hebrew Bible 26, 71, 101, 105, 174
High Priest 41, 102–105, 110, 143
Hillel 11, 22, 38, 63, 179
Holocaust 17, 28, 47
Holy of Holies 73, 102–104, 123, 142
Holy Spirit 67, 71–73, 78–81, 128, 131, 134, 154, 206
Hoshanah Rabbah 11, 132
Huppah 11, 156, 203

Israel Independence Day 16, 28

Jubilee year 20, 88

Kabbalah 11, 25, 132, 153, 184

Ketubah 12, 74–75
Kiddush 12, 173, 185, 197–198
Kittel 12, 37, 130
Kippah 12, 173, 203
Kol Nidrei 12, 106–107
Kosher 12, 48, 55, 142, 203

Lag b'Omer 12, 26
Lent 166, 206
Lulav 12, 120–121, 125, 130, 143, 145

Maccabees 124, 126, 141–145
Matzah 13, 38, 46, 48, 51–53, 55, 60, 62–64
Megillah 13, 164
Menorah 13, 102–104, 143–144, 146, 191
Messianic Jews 13, 49, 101, 153, 182, 202
Mikvah (pl Mikvot) 13, 79, 106
Mishnah 13, 16, 24, 45, 90, 153, 164
Months, Jewish 27, 31

New Year 14, 20, 87–100
New Year for Trees 16, 20, 27, 151–159

Omer 13, 68, 78, 80
Oral law 13, 21–24

Paschal lamb 34–46, 63
Passover 14, 20, 21, 26, 27, 31–66, 68, 90, 123, 128–129, 153, 203–204, 206

INDEX

Pentecost 15, 26, 32, 35, 37, 67–86, 128, 203, 206–207
Persecution 24–25, 46–47, 50, 92, 107, 110, 142, 145, 162, 164–166, 168
Pesach 14, 26, 31–66
Pharisees 14, 21–23, 41, 71, 74, 209, 145, 156, 179
Pilgrim festivals 26, 35, 69, 77, 119
Purim 14, 26, 139, 161–171

Ram's horn 15, 88–89, 92, 96
Recipes:
  Almond cookies 159
  Apple kreplach 138
  Challah bread 192
  Cheese blintzes 83
  Cheesecake 84
  Chicken in orange sauce 56
  Cholent 194
  Cinnamon balls 57
  Coconut pyramids 58
  Gefilte fish 193
  Gingerbread tabernacle 135
  Hamantashen 169
  Honey muffins 99
  Latkes, non–kosher 149
  Lemon and poppy seed cake 170
  Red cabbage 138
  Savoury spinach cheesecake 149
  Sephardi salmon 115
  Tzimmes 98
Repentance 16, 80, 91, 94, 105, 107, 109, 110, 206

Rosh Hashanah 14, 20, 26, 87–100, 106, 130, 206
Ruach ha Kodesh 72

Sabbath 15, 26, 40, 42, 70, 98, 105, 120, 155, 173–200, 203
Sabbatical year 155–156
Sacrifice 21, 35, 37, 42, 46, 92, 102–105, 110, 123, 129, 142
Sadducees 14, 22–23, 40, 70, 145, 179
Safed 11, 25, 47, 132, 153, 184
Salvation 126–127, 130, 204, 206
Sanhedrin 14, 23, 105
Scapegoat 103–104
Second Temple 27, 73, 90, 124
Second Temple Period 102, 126, 163, 177
Seder 14, 38, 45–66, 153–154
Sephardi 15, 24–25, 74, 107, 115, 132, 138
Septuagint 15, 178
Shabbat 15, 26, 41, 108, 142, 173–200, 203
Shammai 15, 22, 179
Shavuot 15, 26, 67–86, 207
Shewbread 102
Shofar 15, 88, 108, 109
Simchat Torah 15, 133
Sinai 68, 73–75, 80, 88, 94–95, 175
Spain 24, 47, 107

Sukkot 15, 26, 119–140, 143, 203, 206
Synagogue 23, 45, 75, 77, 106–107, 132–133, 177–181, 184–185

Tabernacle, the 102, 110, 123, 128
Tabernacles 15, 26, 69, 119–140, 143, 206
Talmud 16, 24, 37, 69, 90, 102, 120, 129, 143, 165
Targum 16, 178
Tashlich 16, 91
Temple 21–24, 27, 35–39, 42, 69–70, 73, 78–80, 92, 102–104, 123–127, 142–144, 178
Teshuvah 16, 105
Tiberias 23, 47
Tishah b'Av 16, 26
Torah 16, 68, 74–77, 80, 101, 104, 106, 124, 131–133, 152, 178, 185, 202
Tu b'Shvat 16, 27, 151–159

Unleavened bread 13, 32, 34, 38–39, 44, 46, 55

Wave offering 40, 68, 70
Wine 33, 39, 44, 55, 131, 154, 164, 173, 184, 187, 189, 197

Yavneh 23, 105, 109, 110
Yeshua 16, 201, 205
Yom h'Atzmaut 16, 28
Yom ha Shoah 17, 28
Yom Kippur 17, 26, 91, 101–117, 130, 138, 206

Jerusalem's Story
A series of Bible studies for individuals or groups

Jerusalem's history can give us a key to the Bible and help us to understand God working in our contemporary world. As more and more Jerusalem takes centre stage in the world's agenda, it becomes increasingly important that Christians should have a good biblical grasp of the significance of this city from Genesis to Revelation. These studies look at both biblical and contemporary themes to link the Bible, history and issues affecting us today. There is also a helpful appendix for leaders giving plenty of additional background material.

Jerusalem's Story
Margot Hodson
ISBN 0 904054 16 0

Olive Press, 30c Clarence Road, St Albans, Herts. AL1 4JJ, UK.
E-mail: olivepress.cmj.org.uk
Web: www.cmj.org.uk/olivep.html
Registered Charity no: 293553

olive press

RESOURCES FROM OLIVE PRESS:

D.I.Y. Passover Kit
Anne Punton

A comprehensive kit especially designed for people with no previous knowledge, showing them how to prepare and conduct a Passover Meal. The pack includes an illustrated service book and a teaching cassette, as well as recipes, table layout and items to make.

Pentecost Beginnings
Margot Hodson

This resource pack is to help churches hold Pentecost celebrations with a Jewish roots approach. It contains everything needed for a weekend including ideas for youth groups, service outlines and recipes for an Israeli lunch.

Harvest Roots

Discover the roots of Harvest at you celebrate the biblical festival of Tabernacles. All the resources for a harvest weekend including service and sermon outlines, harvest supper ideas, teaching for all ages and a music cassette.

Olive Press, 30c Clarence Road, St Albans, Herts. AL1 4JJ, UK.
E-mail: olivepress.cmj.org.uk
Web: www.cmj.org.uk/olivep.html
Registered Charity no: 293553

Thinking of visiting Israel?

Go Shoresh!

Shoresh specialise in tours of Israel that explore the Jewish roots to the Christian faith. All our tours are led by Christian believers and are in comfortable accommodation. We seek to give people the opportunity to visit and understand key biblical sites rather than rush from site to site to 'tick them off.' These are not just educational tours they are a walk with the Lord in his land among his people. Let us help you organise a personalised tour for your church.

For full itineraries and booking forms please contact:

Shoresh Tours,
30c Clarence Road,
St Albans, Herts.
AL1 4JJ, UK.

Tel 01727 810817
Fax 01727 848312
E-mail ShoreshUK@compuserve.com
Web: http://www.cmj.org.uk/shoresh.html